S. Sarbadhicary

A Sojourn in India

Her Manners, Customs, Religion and its Origin

S. Sarbadhicary

A Sojourn in India
Her Manners, Customs, Religion and its Origin

ISBN/EAN: 9783337259914

Printed in Europe, USA, Canada, Australia, Japan

Cover: Foto ©Andreas Hilbeck / pixelio.de

More available books at **www.hansebooks.com**

A SOJOURN IN INDIA:

HER MANNERS, CUSTOMS, RELIGION AND ITS ORIGIN.

BY

S. SARBADHICARY, F.S.Sc.

Editor of " The Speeches on Early Marriage, etc.," and Author of " A Sojourn in the United States of America ;" Late Manager of Western Union Telegraph Office, Broad Channel, Long Island, U.S. America ; Member of the University College of Edinburgh, and that of the Hon. Society of Gray's Inn, London.

LONDON :

PRINTED AND PUBLISHED BY ARLISS ANDREWS, MUSEUM STREET.

1890.

Preface.

———

I HAVE the pleasure of writing the preface of this interesting book of Mr. Sarbadhicary, whose style of writing impresses me with the idea that he has received very good education.

The Earl of Aberdeen, of England, told him, " your book is excee dingly interesting ; the composition is very good so I shall read it with great pleasure. I beg to reciprocate my good wishes to you in giving you a cheque of five pounds."

Earl Compton, Professor J. Kirkpatrick, M.A., LL.B.,* University College of Edinburgh, Professor Elphinstone, M.A., Barrister-at-Law, of London, Dr. J. Carment, LL.D., an eminent lawyer of Edinburgh, Colonel Davies, and many others of England and Scotland have spoken very highly of his former works. When they reached this country I saw in *The Electric Age*, a widely-circulated journal, a very flattering notice, in which Mr. Wm. J. Dealy, manager of the largest telegraph office in the world, remarked, " I marvel at Mr. Sarbadhicary's book ; it is in many respects one of the most interesting works I have ever read. He is a scholar and evidently a man of grand character. He is worthy of encouragement," The editor himself remarks, "the book has been written in vivid English style." Another journal, named *The Critic*, remarks, " one of the most

———

* This gentleman certifies that Mr. Sarbadhicary has written two essays on historical subjects exhibiting his best English knowledge.

interesting books we have ever read is ' A Sojourn in the
United States of America, by S. Sarbadhicary.' Should
he return to New York, the London *Times* would com-
mission him to write a series of papers on the States,
which will be more strikingly original than the articles
of its commissioner."

The first chapter of the present work was submitted to
Professor Elphinstone, M.A., who said, "your manuscript
does not require any correction."

Reverend Filian, graduate of the Chicago University,
inquired of Mr. Sarbadhicary, "How did you learn such
good English? I can honestly say that few English and
American graduates can write better style. You not only
have very good English knowledge but a great descriptive
power." My own opinion is the same. But when I consider that the author was a poor Indian orphan of high
caste, who received no help from his relatives who usurped
all his defenceless property and left him to combat with
poverty and starvation, I can say his work is unrivalled.

Goldsmith says, " the loss of fortune simply serves to
increase the pride of the worthy," and this gentleman,
profitting by the idea, rose from orphanage and destitution,
to the position of one of the most eminent authors.

During his infancy, several attempts were made to
induce him to liquor, but he resolutely declined the overtures of the drunkards and lead the life of a total
abstainer.

My statement will excite the curiosity of the public, to
know how Mr. Sasi (which is his first name) could bring
himself up. To satisfy their eagerness I beg to say that
the premature death of his father, when only one year old
and the loss of his paternal property (a mango grove, rice
fields, an unfinished building and moveable household

property) left him dependent on his maternal uncle, who nobly sheltered him beneath his hospitable roof at Mohespore, a village in Bengal, East India. At five years of age he was sent to the village school where he made considerable improvement in vernacular studies. The fear of a tiger, not an unfrequent visitor of that locality, the incessant showers of rain, the thunderstorm, and the knee-deep mud could seldom furnish an obstacle to the unfailing regularity with which he attended his school.

His scholastic studies however, were disturbed by the death of his uncle, who suffered from an attack of a lingering disease and breathed his last, leaving to the aspiring infant, Natma a village, two gardens, rice-fields, cattle and a building. Their management was entrusted to several of his relatives who appropriated the property and left the boy destitute.

At the age of seven he went to Calcutta and was admitted in the Queen's College. The progress of his studies was further arrested by a dangerous attack of spleen-fever. When dying, he was handed to a native physician, who took off his clothes and held a piece of burning wood on his belly under the pretence of killing the " alive pilla " (spleen). He was subsequently handed to another murderer who thrusted red-hot iron into his belly. Instead of killing the pilla, they inflicted such wounds the scars of which will never be removed from the belly of Mr. Sarbadhicary. When the appeal to gods and goddesses and the attempts of native physicians proved useless an Englishman cured him. On recovery, he commenced his studies at Kishnaghur, the expenses of which, in spite of his close connection with Prince Digumber Mittra and the princely family of Shava Bazar, Calcutta, were defrayed by his own acquired money.

He is a liberal and "home ruler" and has addressed meetings in support of his views both in Edinburgh and in London.

The *Edinburgh Daily Review, Edinburgh Evening Dispatch* and *Scotsman* reported that on the 30th of May, a very short speech of Mr. Sarbadhicary, to the electors of the Southern division of Edinburgh, under the chairmanship of Right Hon. W. McWan, was most enthusiastically received by the audience. Another short address delivered by him on the Irish Question, in Clerkenwell, London, under the chairmanship of Right Hon. Rowlands, M.P., (not to be confounded with Right Hon. Rowlands, M.P., Treasurer of Gray's Inn,) was received with equal enthusiasm.

My views echo the prophecy of princess Burra Rani, of Shava Bazar, Calcutta, who predicted that "persevering, as Sarbadhicary is, he will cut a prominent figure on some future day."

I sincerely hope that this book of my talented friend, should have a larger sale than those of its predecessors.

E. T. PARDEE,

W. Chief,

Syracuse,   Main Office,

New York,   Western Union Tel. Co.

U.S. America,

January, 1890.

Contents.

CHAPTER VIII.

CHAPTER IX.

CHAPTER X.

CHAPTER XI.

[CHAPTER XII.

A SOJOURN IN INDIA.

CHAPTER I.

My Departure from Calcutta—The description and fall of Pandua—
The Description of Burdwan—Allahabad and Benares.

(Having promised several of my American friends that I
would write "A Sojourn in India" on my return to England,
I hereby beg to fulfil my promise.)

The death of my maternal uncle (who nobly sheltered
me beneath his hospitable roof) and other domestic difficulties which followed, so materially affected my health,
that but for the kindly intervention of a merciful Providence, my own life might have ended here and these
pages would have remained unwritten. The series of
misfortunes which followed the event, impressed me with
the idea that a blight had fallen over my fortune. A few
thoughtless friends advised me to repair my prospects by a
wealthy marriage, but to marry, to enjoy a nice house and
a garden with grass plot and lake, a carriage, and other
auxiliaries to domestic felicity on the one hand, and may
be subjected to a domineering mother-in-law on the other
are so alien to my views, that I indignantly declined to
entertain the idea. I was but fifteen when I left Calcutta,
October, 1876. The only luggage I carried was a carpet
bag, a piece of thin linen cloth and a few shirts. The
cold season was approaching, and I was not accustomed
to severe weather in Calcutta which was so mild that a

woollen shirt is sufficient to keep a person warm throughout
the year, and I imagined that the cold of other parts of
India would not exceed that of Calcutta.

I crossed the Hughly River to Howrah, where I was
introduced to some persons about to leave for Patna. They
inquired with kindly interest of me, my intentions and
my projected movements. Uncertain where to go and
unwilling to acquaint strangers with my real destination, I
mentioned Pandua. They afterwards proved to be very
good people and walked with me to the Howrah Railway
Station. We bought our tickets, went to the train and
reached Pandua, once the seat of a Hindu Rajah and
strongly fortified by a trench five miles in circumference.
Pandua has a tower 120 feet high, which commands a
grand view of the surrounding orchards, mango groves,
arborial gardens and rice fields. It has defied the rain
and storm of the tropical climate of Bengal for a period of
500 years, and will yet resist for scores of years both time
and weather. Singularly enough, the downfall of the last
of its princes may be attributed to a battle for a cow. On
the birth of a child of the prince, the event was celebrated
with great pomp. The festivity lasted several days, and
thousands of guests were most liberally entertained. Among
them was a Mahommedan named Munshi Mirdulla. A
feast of such importance in the eyes of a Mahommedan
would be incomplete without a nice beefsteak; so repugnant
is it to the Hindu feeling that a man of high caste is more
willing to die than see a *melacha* (the Hindus call all others
who are not Hindus *melachas*, or barbarians) take beef in
his neighbourhood. The Mahommedan who was the
Persian translator of the Court could hardly resist his
temptation : he killed a cow, and for fear of detection buried
the unconsumed portion. But a pack of quick-scented
animals (jackals) appeared on the spot at sun-down, disin-
terred the carcase, and feasted on it the whole night. The
wrath of the Hindus at a discovery so offensive to their
religious feelings admitted no bounds. The terrified
Munshi appealed to the people of his own sect for help.
The Mahommedans and the Hindus ranged themselves for
battle and fought with desperate valour. When the latter

were outnumbered, the former defiled the water of a tank which the Hindus used for drinking and cooking by throwing beef* and starved the enemy, so the Mahommedans won the battle and commemorated the victory by erecting the tower. Most of the Hindus were killed or reduced to slavery, their houses were razed to the ground, and the animosities of the race-distinction were perpetuated. The Munshi was placed on the throne, but conscience-stricken with the thought that he had purchased territory and dignity by guilt, and stung by the reflection that a little prudence would have avoided the sad catastrophe, and that he might have enjoyed a long peaceful life, receiving his rice and salt from the hand of the reigning prince, sought to atone for his offence by cruel self-inflicted penance and incessant prayer until he died.

In a tank, between 40 and 45 feet deep, there is a tame alligator, which always obeyed the call of a fakeer to whom he was accustomed ; when hungry, he hesitated to leave the presence of the fakeer until food was served.

We reached Burdwan at 12 o'clock p.m. The only passengers who got in were two ladies and a young man in English dress. One of the men in our compartment, dressed in Indian costume, passed the remark, "Native Christian." The youth, as it appeared to me, tainted with all the defects from which precocious, half-educated lads of quick parts are seldom free, at once reported to the station-master, and begged the removal of the man. The station-master took up the cause and strove to remove him, when I made an apology on his behalf, and guaranteed his future good behaviour.

Legend tells us that in antiquity the daughter of one of the princes of Burdwan, who was named Bidda (Learning), was so well educated that she challenged any male individual to controversy in any branch of literature or science. In case he succeeded, she would marry him, if not, she would not marry at all. This vow affected her mother so much that she shed tears, as an

---

* The cow is held sacred and when killed the flesh is the most abhorrent of all objects to the eyes of a Hindu.

unmarried person is subject, by a Hindu custom, to many social disabilities.   Her literary fame astounded every person in India, and at length attracted the attention of a youth named Sundra, of Kanchipore.   He had extremely limited education, but this defect was amply compensated by his quality in other directions.   He was a good mechanic, a fine horseman, and a beautiful archer.   By a subterranean excavation, Sundra made his way incognito into the chambers of Bidda, and the young pair, being of the same caste, same creed, and of princely origin, were united by a marriage which was celebrated with great pomp and festivity.*

Here is a nice menagerie, wherein are placed two alligators in a tank which is constantly resorted to by a rhinoceros, but he never received any injury from the destructive animals.

The train started from Burdwan, and reached Ranegunge, which, being situated in an open extensive plain, with its pretty whitewashed buildings, with geeen painted windows, the busy coaleries, clustered columns and huts, interspersed with shrubs and trees, present a picturesque appearance in the valley of the fantastic Damudar. †

From the train we could see distinctly the Grand Trunk Road, which runs from Bengal to Peshawar.   Formerly tigers lurked there in great numbers, and on the approach of night all traffic was stopped by the dread of the Royal Bengal man-eater.   Now, perhaps on account of the noise of the train, they prowl in the neighbouring jungle, but never make their appearance on the road.   Their neighbours, the santhals, are the most successful destroyers of the tigers.   The former fight with their arrows, the latter with their paws, armed with cruel retractile claws, but human intelligence invariably succeeds in overcoming brute strength and ferocity.

The train passed through Bankipore, and arrived at Allahabad, which is situated at the confluence of the Jumna (a sacred river) and the Ganges (the most sacred of rivers).

* I get the account from a book published by Bharut Chunder, a courtier of the prince of Kishnaghur.

† A river subject to sudden overflows.

It is a matter of common belief that if a person can drown himself in the latter, he goes to heaven. The eternal river, as it is sometimes called, fertilizes many valleys and fields. It is the highway of traffic throughout the year, and forms one of the chief sources of the income of India. The Jumna, with its teeming animal life, the crocodiles, the tortoises, and rich flora, presents the most interesting sight to zoologists. The crystal blue water rolls nimbly between the craggy banks, and subsequently obtains another name, Kalidah.*

I drove to a pretty villa on the banks of the Ganges, where the bloom and the beauty of its parterres furnish a lovely picture. In a little tub a number of parthenopes being placed, moved about with great agility. I was furnished with an introductory note to the owner of the house, whose judicious selection of the building as much evidenced his taste as his management did his capacity. After some refreshment, I took leave of my kind host, who hospitably invited me to stay a day or two. I caught the 9 p.m. down train for Benares.

Benares is a holy city, immortalized by the vivid description of Macaulay. It is the chief seat of Sanskrit learning. Pundits of Lahore Oriental College are the scholars of the noble institutions of this sacred city. The priestly caste, the temples, the Ganges, the bulls, and the monkeys, are perhaps the most notable of the many sacred things here. It is affirmed by popular opinion that earthquakes happen only in cities where the weight of sin is very great, and so it is maintained that this city, being entirely exempted from sin, will never be subjected to even the most moderate of shocks. Believing that beatific fate awaits all who die here, people from all parts of India journey to Benares, with a view to be transferred to heaven by dying in so propitious a death-place. I learned from a friend of mine that an old man from Bangalore

* It is said that Krishna, the incarnation of Vishnu, Indian God, one day grazed his cows on the banks of Kalidah, at Brindabun. Some cows and a shepherd boy were killed by drinking water which had been maliciously poisoned by a large serpent. Krishna, after two hours' hard fighting, defeated and killed the animal.

went there to die, but fearing that whilst absent from the city in his daily walk, he might die suddenly elsewhere and so lose the benefit of the sanctity of Benares, he mutilated himself. One day his desire for a ride was so great that he ordered his servant to bring a saddled horse. The servant, in obedience to his master's direction, obtained a horse, but the rider, after proceeding some miles, was thrown and killed. From the surrounding country, Benares presents a magnificent view to the delighted eye of the traveller. It is the chief seat of Hindu theology, philosophy, logic, science, and jurisprudence. It has the highest appellate religious jurisdiction over Mithila, Nuddea, and Dravira, which, in return, exercise jurisdiction over other cities and towns. The pundits are profound Sanskrit scholars, and have given us to understand that the city is really the city of Saraswattee (goddess of Learning), as Athens was the city of Minerva. Benares holds the thread of learning and civilization in India, as Athens did in Europe. Cicero says, " Recollect, Quintus, that you govern the Greeks who civilized all nations by teaching them mildness and humanity, and to whom Rome is indebted for all the knowledge she possesses." An author tells us, " Now the Athens which civilized Europe had in her turn been civilized by Benares ; the city of Saraswattee, has the precedence over the city of Minerva. The Hindus are acknowledged as the first to have started in the race of civilization." We actually see that Cicero and Atticus went to Athens to study eloquence and its source, and Lycurgus and Pythagoras went to India to learn law and philosophy, with a view to assimilate those of Greece ; whilst India has invited the greatest men of the greatest country, who ostensibly admitted the superiority of the Indian system of study ; decidedly our ancestors' deeds rest beyond the range of our criticism. We modern Indians are very short-sighted, so we often undervalue our forefathers' institutions, but great statesmen like Edmund Burke and Mr. John Bright—alas! now dead—men of universally admitted knowledge, capacity, and foresight, admired Indian institutions of antiquity. Sir William Jones, a great Sanskrit scholar, visited Benares, and was so astonished to hear even ordinary students converse in

Sanskrit with such dignified style, with such judicious diction and logical cogency, that he regretted his separation from such educated companions and noble institutions, in the same way as Julian did when a royal message from Rome disturbed his academical life, inviting him to exchange the life of a school for that of a palace. I lived in a Hindu hotel in Benares, and left it for Cawnpore.

CHAPTER II.

Cawnpore—Patiala—Mahabharata—Delhi—Agra and Cashmere.

Nana Sahib and Cawnpore are so strangely associated with each other and so painfully impressed upon British memory, that the name of one is sure to recall that of the other. Nana was but a lad of twenty, when the mutiny broke out. He had an ample share of bull-dog courage which never flinched from any danger. He might have heightened his glory to epic heroism, even in the opinion of those antagonistic to his views, had he openly challenged the English and disputed the palm of military prowess. He had undoubted capacity, aided by an unblushing face and specious lying tongue, adamantine heart and tiger-like ferocity. He strongly asserted that he would be able to form an Indian Empire which would outshine the glory of that of his renowned forefather, the great Sevajee. Accordingly he went to Delhi and forced the nominal Emperor to aid him; he induced the Queen of Jhansi to fight on his behalf, and kindled the conflagration of mutiny by a false rumour that the British intended to destroy the caste of both the Hindus and the Mahommedans. Such a fanatic can never be found outside the pale of a madhouse. Since the unlucky event, (mutiny), his name has been associated with that terrible dark massacre which we can never name, even at this distant day, without shuddering horror, combined with a tribute to the noble services of the arms of the avengers.

At Cawnpore lived a class of people called Bengalees. They were the natives of Lower Bengal. One of their forefathers, Rajah Deva Pal Deva enjoyed the whole of the Indian territory and military glory during the ninth century, but since then, the Bengalee having greatly degenerated, has never assumed a conspicuous position or any position in Indian history. He may make a competent lawyer, doctor, clerk, but is never likely to distinguish himself as a captain in the army or navy. Some of this class settling in Cawnpore, raised themselves to affluence by rendering faithful services to the British Government. On the outbreak of the mutiny, they concealed themselves in a small building, to avoid the ferocity of the mutineers. The place of their concealment was revealed to Nana, who summoned them and accused them for giving information to the English. Accordingly the sentence of death and mutilation was passed on them. But Lord Canning, in spite of empty treasury, and mutinied troops, sent General Havelock, with a handful of soldiers by land and a small boat with an army by water. Nana seeing he was about to be attacked both by land and water, ran away; his troops having lost their leader, submitted, and order was restored.

I left Cawnpore for Patiala, and reached the residence of Babu Avinash Chunder Chatterjee, the Director of Public Instruction. He was away on his holiday, but I was very kindly admitted by Babu Birashur Chatterjee, the principal of the Patiala College, who united a commanding presence to a handsome face and melodious voice. I was temporarily appointed a private tutor to the children of the former gentleman. This was a turning point in the incidents of my life. In Bengal, I was a student, then a traveller, and here I found myself a teacher. As soon as I received the first month's pay, I bought some warm clothes and set out for Delhi.

Under the name of Delhi are comprised the three cities, India Prastha, Mediæval Delhi, and Modern Delhi. Tradition affirms that there lived a prince named Bharat, who conquered the whole of India and transmitted it to his posterity. The inheritance, at length descended to his great great grandson, Santanu, who during his old age desired to marry a young maiden. No one, however, would give his daughter to the old man, unless his boy, Vishma, guaranteed that he would devote himself to a life of celibacy. To gratify the doting father, the lad vowed as to the idea of his leading a single life. The marriage was completed, and a son named Vichitravirya was born of Santanu. Vichitravirya had three children, of whom the second, named Pandu, succeeded to the territory. On his death, the sovereignty descending to his children was disputed by those of the eldest brother, Dhritarastra, whose eldest son, Durjodhana, was a lad of bad principles, turbulent temper, insatiable cupidity and implacable malevolence. Early feuds among the cousins led to the banishment of the Pandavas, (children of Pandu*). They selected Baranabat as the place of their banishment, but the tyrant, Durjodhana sent there a number of working men, with instructions to erect a building, and to receive the children with their mother Kunti, and, anon set it on fire. The brothers, honest and incapable of deceit, so unsuspecting of it in others entered the building. At night, when asleep, it was fired. A providential inspiration had induced Bidura, the second uncle, to dig a subterranean passage. Bhima, the second brother, who was the strongest man in the world, managed to carry the remaining inmates through the passage. When they crossed the tunnel, Bhima met Hidimba, the cannibal prince of that region. In a desperate duel, the former killed the latter and married his sister, Hidimbi, the imperious and reckless vixen who succeeded to the throne of her deceased brother. Bhima with his brothers and the mother went to Ekachakra, a village where they all resided in disguise. Here Bhima killed another cannibal named Baka.

Hearing the Draupadi Sayambara (marriage) would be celebrated in Panchala (Punjab), the Pandavas reached that territory, and fairly won the girl. A reconciliation having been effected with Durjodhana through the medium of King Drupada, the father of the bride, the Pandavas were allowed to return to Hasthinapore. They gave a

---

* I very much regret to say that for want of space I cannot write this legendary incident in detail, but I sincerely hope that on some future occasion I shall be able to give a full account of this ancient story.

grand banquet on account of a great festivity (horse sacrifice), and invited all princes, potentates, and kings of the then known world, who did their homage to the Pandava chief, Judishthira. This spectacle was more than enough for Durjodhana, the Kaurava chief, to bear. It broke his spirit, soured his temper, and ultimately impaired his health. Having lost his head and heart, he strove hard to banish the Pandavas again. He challenged Judishthira to play a game of chess with him, on condition that his maternal uncle, named Sakuni, to whom forgery, chicanery and other evil practices were quite familiar, should conduct the play. In this unfair contest the sincere-hearted man lost everything. The five brothers were treated as slaves in the public durbar. Draupadi, the wife, a lady of stainless virtue and reputation, and who, according to Indian custom, kept always inside her palace, was caught by the hair and brought to the presence of the whole court. During this critical conjuncture, the pious Judishthira submitted patiently to the galling restraints, bore such cruel indignities with external serenity, and forgave offences which moved Bhima to such resentment as to vow, "I shall kill the monster Dushashana," second son of Dhritarashtra, "on some future day," and Draupadi vowed with dishevelled hair, "I will never regulate my hair until retribution falls on the perpetrator." But the devout Judishthira alone could hide the indignity under the show of stoical serenity. The sympathy of the whole court was with the Pandavas and Durjodhana had no strength of mind to stop the evil tide, of which he himself was the author, and to which the whole family would be victims.

At length Judishthira was banished with all his brothers for thirteen years. They travelled in disguise for miles, and at length reached a beautiful spot, having a majestic mountain in front, with crystal lake, streams and trees, the branches of which were bent down by the weight of delicious fruits and blooming flowers. They pitched their humble tent, fetched fruits from the neighbouring jungle, and appeased their hunger, and very comfortably slept on the bed of leaves. Their cousin Durjodhana, accompanied by the greatest archers, including Karna, with great magnificence pitched his gigantic tents in front, but a gandharva having done the same, provoked his haughty neighbour, Durjodhana, who ordered him to withdraw, and was maddened with the contumelious reply, "Come and execute your order." A battle was fought, and he was taken prisoner with all his troops. The melancholy news reached the propitious ears of Judishthira, who forthwith ordered his third brother, Arjuna, to release the tyrant, for, said he, "unless he is liberated, the gandharva would tauntingly declare the Kurava chief was taken prisoner in the face of the Pandavas." Accordingly Arjuna set Durjodhana and his troops free. The latter, with heavy heart, returned to his court.

Soon after this event, the Pandavas went to the territory of Prince Birat who was subsequently invaded by Durjodhana with a mighty army, and was dispersed by Arjuna alone. On the completion of full thirteen years, the Pandavas returned to Hastinapore, but nothing diminished the claim of the Kauravas to the fovour of Judishthira. He embraced them heartily, and proposed the terms of peace, but to no purpose. At last war was declared, and the battles were fought on the vast plain of Kurukshetra. Arjuna, at the first onset, gallantly upheld the flag of victory, and the timid Durjodhana passed from haughty apathy to abject terror, but at the close of the day, Vishma the commander-in-chief of the Kaurava army, killed 10,000 troops of Arjuna, and returned victorious to his camp. He valiantly fought for nine days, and on the tenth he fell on the battle-field, and with his dying words said to Durjodhana that he never ceased to regret to the last moment of his long life of prosperity and success the unlucky war, and requested him to compromise. Durjodhana neglected to profit by such laudable advice; he continued the war, and was killed with his ninety-nine brothers and other relatives. The sight of the dreary marshes of field and neighbouring desolate villages awakened many a sad recollection in the heart of their descendants who could but deplore the want of strength of mind of Durjodhana for which he lost the inheritance and life so prematurely.

Modern Delhi is but a few miles from Hastinapore.

During the reign of the Emperor Kutubooddeen it was about thirty miles in circumference. About five miles distant stands the majestic Kutub-minar, which is about 300 feet high. It is divided into five stories, every one of which has a projecting balcony, supported upon rich stone brackets. It has 376 stone steps. Some say it was built by a Hindu prince to enable his daughter to see the Jumna and the Ganges every morning at sun-rise. The iron pillar is the oldest of all monuments. It is of solid metal, sixty feet long and sixteen broad. It weighs seventeen tons. It attests the engineering capacity of the ancient Hindus and commemorates their glory. Some say it was erected during the reign of the Pandavas, and others during the reign of Deva Pal Deva. Its foundation is so deep beneath the ground that the pundits said to a prince of the Tomara Dynasty, "if he did not interfere with the pillar which rests on the head of Vasuki (the goddess of snakes), he would transmit his throne to posterity," but doubting the veracity of this statement, he displaced it, and found blood at the end, when he bitterly regretted, and attempted to fix it again, but it was too late. He was subsequently killed.

I greatly enjoyed the Delhi-Durbar, where Her Majesty, the Queen was proclaimed, with great enthusiasm, the Empress of India. The Governor-General delivered a number of addresses to the princes, chiefs and the nobles. When the Durbar was complete, I was advised by a gentleman to learn telegraphy; accordingly he sent me with an introductory note to Agra.

Delhi, 7th January, 1877.
Dear Sir,
I hereby beg to send you a young lad, named Babu Sasi Bhushan Sarbadhicary. He is honest, active and intelligent. I shall be highly obliged if you kindly appoint him as a telegraph probationer.
Yours truly,
To Babu Prasana, JADU NATH GOSH.
Coomer Chukerbutty,
Shajadimundi,
Agra.

On my arrival at Agra, I appeared in the preliminary examination. I passed and joined the telegraph school.

When I was considered competent, Mr. Rutherford, the telegraph superintendent, with a strong recommendation, sent me to the line.

I joined my new calling in February, 1877, at Delhi. I worked telegraphy for four months only, when, in hopes of getting a post of better salary, I started for the province of Cashmere.

Srinaggur is the capital of Cashmere. Jhelum, a noble river, intersects the city. Cashmere has about 68.000 square miles, and over a million of population. From time immemorial it has been governed by the Hindu princes, but at intervals the predatory Tartars disturbed their quiet possession. Akbar was the first Moghul emperor who conquered and added it to his domain. During the period of the greatest glory of the Sikhs, Maharajah Golab Singh, the grandfather of the present reigning prince, was appointed governor of Jummu as a reward for his gallantly upholding the flag of victory against Akbar Khan. Golab Singh at last extended his sway from Jummu to Ladak, with a large revenue.

Cashmere has several fine gardens. It is famous as the seat of the manufacture of shawls. Under Prince Ranabir, property was more secure than formerly. From Jummu to Cashmere I travelled on horseback. On my arrival I was appointed temporarily in the silk manufactory.

CHAPTER III.

Lahore—My Career in Bombay—My Journey to Simla and Ludhiana.

I subsequently set out for Lahore and was temporarily engaged in the Railway Offices. Having made a little money, I joined the Lahore District School and passed the entrance examination (1878), with a scholarship which enabled me to continue my studies in the Government and Oriental Colleges and in the junior and senior law classes over two years. The Superintendent of the Oriental College gave me a very kind certificate :—

"This is to certify that Babu S. B. Sarbadhicary has been a student in this Institution for the last two years. He is an active and diligent young man and is well aquainted with the Sanskrit language and literature.
GURU PERSHAD,
Oriental College,
Officiating Superintendent."

Dr. Leitner the late principal of the Government College gave me a very gratifying certificate. In the law class our prescribed text was—(1.) Civil Law including Hindu and Mahommedan Law. (2.) Penal Code and Criminal Procedure. (3.) Civil Procedure Code and Tagore Law. (4). Evidence and Contract Acts. (5.) Registration and Limitation Acts and judicial interpretation. These are the principal books but a number of minor acts are attached to every one of the branches. I studied all the prescribed books but scholarship being the only source of my income it proved inadequate to defray all my expenses. Accordingly I suspended my studies.

During Maharajah Runjit Singh's reign Lahore the capital of the Punjab, was the most prosperous city. It has a strong fort at a distance of two miles from which runs the Ravi River a branch of the Indus (Attock) from which the name India is derived. I went to Rawul Pindi one of the chief towns of the Punjab and established an elementary school. Whilst still struggling to make the school a success I was requested by a friend to give the school to him. On refusal, a society was established and when I was requested to comply with the wishes of the society, I submitted the school to it, desiring the society to perpetuate the Institution. I eventually left Rawul Pindi for Bombay.

Bombay is on an island, the hills of which are decorated with beautiful trees with rich fruits and exquisite flowers. Contiguous to the General Post Office, stands the Central Telegraph Office, in a building not far from which is the signaller's quarter where the operators, like the telegraphists of Madeira, resided free of charge.

I lived in a building situated in the interior of the city and passed the preliminary examination. On entering the Civil Training School I worked for the final which was of a difficult nature. Three years' study is necessary for a student in Otukmund to qualify himself for the examination. There are but four branches, namely, Electricity, Magnetism ; Knowledge of Instrument Traffic Code, Foreign Guide, Indian Guide ; Receiving and Signalling. Mr. Alfred Perkins a most able and popular officer, was the chief of our seminary. Several of the candidates appeared on different occasions and having failed, I became nervously anxious on my own account and worked with redoubled vigour. The energy displayed by our excellent instructor could hardly be exaggerated. He encouraged all his students in every possible way. The day of the examination battle drew near and Mr. Alfonso S. A. superintendent, reputed an extremely strict examiner, made his appearance. At the close of the examination, we went away with all the glee of American

schoolboys who leave the monotony of school life a harsh
teacher and quarrelsome companions to spend a Merry
Christmas with the friends and relatives of a happy home
circle. Mr. Alfonso being transferred was succeeded
by Mr. Parrot a most popular official, the superintending
telegraph master who according to official rules, sent
our papers to Calcutta. In a few weeks a very satisfactory
result reached Mr. Parrot who invited me to his office, gave
me ten pounds informing me that I passed with credit in
three subjects and in the remaining branch I obtained just
enough marks to pass. I was placed in an office named
Mombadevie on a salary of £6 a month. Eventually in
a general examination having done well I was transferred
to the Punjab on a salary of £7 10s. a month.

Simla is a cool and salubrious place situated on the
summit of the Himalaya mountain. Sabatu, Kasauli and
Simla combined, present a grand view to the traveller.
The hilly ranges rise one above the other, the summits
of which are crowned with perpetual snow, the roads
ascending and descending with alternating levels. The
only conveyance admitted in Simla is a jhapan carried
on the shoulders of the coolies but horses can be hired at
moderate charges. From Bombay *en route* to Simla I
paid a visit to Mr. Bignell the superintendent of telegraph at
Ambala where I hired a *dak gari* from the Post Office and
set out on my jonrney. Hardly had I left the town for a
couple of hours when I found an isolated mud-house
thatched with straw, on the premises of which a huge
elephant was fastened to a sycamore-like tree. I asked the
driver why an elephant was kept in that desolate land.
The man said pointing out an open space " this is a river
the bed of which is dry throughout the year but when
subject to inundations its current is so strong as to cut even
a reed in twain and wash away men, ekka and *dak-gari*, so a
competent man sufficiently skilful to declare the precise
moment of the inundation is kept to stop the traffic and
convey it by means of the elephant which being a robust
animal is not easily washed away. At sun-rise I reached
Kalka and through the help of the telegraph master a
tonga was hired. This is a light conveyance drawn by a

c

pair of stalwart mountain horses which can climb to the topmost pinnacle of a mountain with steady steps. Here I found another signaller named Sweeni an Englishman. We travelled together until we arrived at a village named Dogshai where both being thirsty I went to the neighbouring waterfall and quenched my thirst by drinking cold water and my companion to a coffee-house provided by a Mahommedan whose conduct was greatly criticised for furnishing coffee to a Kafir (all those who are not Mahommedans are called Kafirs) on a festive day. On reaching Simla, we assumed our duties and its accompanying liabilities. We had a number of instruments to which were attached lightning-dischargers to protect the signaller whilst at key.   Occasionally I went to the Sabatu telegraph master and a commissariat official named Rameshawur Babu from whom I always enjoyed a genial welcome. The sedateness of his deportment, the regularity of his life, the liberality of his habit, delighted the austere moralists of Simla. I proposed here I would establish an elementary school but local prejudice and the absence of funds proved almost insurmountable difficulties.

At length a gentleman promised me a room, another a few students and a third a teacher thus all obstacles by degrees were overcome. The number of pupils gradually increased. Whilst the enterprise was about to be made a success, I was ordered to proceed to Ludhiana. I made proper arrangement for the maintenance of the school during my absence and left Simla with David another signaller for the above station. We journeyed the distance of 300 miles by *tonga dak-gari* and rail respectively and reached the station of our destination. Two English signallers named Toohey and Cumber went to the railway station in hopes of accompanying us to the office. The only means by which they could recognise us were our warm clothes of the hilly country but the fact of our having changed the dress defeated their kind intentions. David drove away to the office and I to the house of a Bengalee a man with a brilliant wit and ready invention, but with exceptionally singular opinions, who believes that no Asiatic can ever hope to reach England because he has never seen a native of Ludhiana leave it for this country. The journey having proved too much to my chronic eyes, I went to the hospital instead of the office.

Ludhiana is situated on the bank of the Sutlej. In 1620 it was conquered by the Rais of Rajkote. Runjit, the lion of the Punjab, pulled the prince down and set up Rajah Bhag Sing of Jhind. Soon after Runjit's death, the English occupied it. In antiquity Ludhiana was the favourite resort of the princes and Nawabs. The descendants of Shah Shoojaho, Dost Mahommed and Yar Mahommed can still be seen.

When my eyes were recovered, I commenced to work in the office under Mr. Wilson the telegraph master whose delicacy of feeling and generosity of sentiment were well calculated to win the esteem even of a stranger. We all including Mr. Wilson and his children lived in the signallers' quarter. Beside all those above mentioned we had another signaller named Murray a young man of great ambition. He fought with the soldiers of Ambala, and with their S. A. superintendent by wire, fought with other signallers at home and in the office cleared his official work by his superabundant activity, although none liked to stay in the office when he was there. He arrived at a stage of life (17 years) when youth could no longer be pleaded as an excuse for a fault. In the evening we walked together after instructing our servants as to the place where we should sleep at night. Sometimes we slept on the veranda and sometimes in the garden as the prickly heat did not allow us to sleep indoors but during the hurricane called *andhi*, we were forced to go in. When I fulfilled my mission by clearing the work I was re-transferred to Simla. I joined the office and had hardly worked for a fortnight, when I was ordered to proceed to Kalka. Here the English system of working was introduced. The Government by this change intended to base other offices on the same principle, abolish the post of Director-General and make the Post-Master-General the supreme authority for both the telegraph and the post offices, as in this country. The amalgamation of two departments would save £3,500 a year. Whilst at Simla Mr. Doneghey,

the S. A. superintendent of a Simla office having promised
me in a private interview, the acceptance of my resignation without the usual ceremony, I secured a passage by
the Rebatino Italian mail steamer from Bombay to Genoa
and resigned.

CHAPTER IV.

Kalka—Amritsur—Rawul Pindi Attack—Jamrud—The Afghan War—My Journey to Sibi and Bolan Pass.

I left Kalka on the 4th of October for Amritsur the wealthiest and most populous city of the Punjab. The famous place of worship called the Golden Temple is situated in a tank, erected in the centre of Amritsur ; when the mellow effulgence of the setting sun reflects the golden dome the beauty of this edifice makes a lasting impression on our minds. It was erected by Maharajah Runjit Singh. When visiting India the Prince of Wales in ignorance of the local custom that no one is permitted to enter a building dedicated to religion wearing shoes violated the rule but on being informed of the prevailing custom, the Prince immediately conformed and won universal golden opinion. (I mention this upon approved information, but I cannot guarantee the accuracy of the statement.) There is a tower dedicated to Athal Rai who is said to have been sternly reprimanded by his father Har Govinda, for raising a child from the dead. Har Govinda recommended his son to display his supernatural power in purity of doctrine and purity of life rather than by a miracle whereupon the son declared that if he erred in giving life to one he would take it away from another. So saying he prostrated himself and rose no more.* From Amritsur I went to the healthful post of Rawul Pindi. It is divided by a small stream called Leh which according to the season presents three feet

---

*Cunningham's " Sikhs."

deep water or a perfectly dry bed. The surrounding country is mountainous and the fords are extremely dangerous and although the water seldom exceeds the shallowness mentioned, the stream is a most rapid one. Once a foreigner regardless of caution attempted to cross without a guide but the strength of the current overturned him and his body was not discovered until three days afterwards. Paying a flying visit to Muree I went to Attock where a gentleman named Gopal Babu Godown Gomastha resided. Whilst at Rawul Pindi I was often invited to see him but the nature of my duty did not allow me to avail myself of his kind invitation. I crossed the Attock River and started for Peshawur which is the limit of the Indian territory and which can be visited by the persons of the highest caste without being subject to excommunication. From Peshawur I went to Jamrud where I was much impressed by the mountainous grandeur of the Khyber Pass the opening of which, flanked by two sentinel-like isolated snowy hills, forms the entrance of the narrow gorge which barely allows two horsemen to travel abreast. Here one day, perhaps within our lifetime, history may record that a modern Leonidas may check the inroad of the hordes of present Xerxes on the Indian side of the Asiatic Thermopylæ. At Jamrud the Afghan women, almost as fair as the English, descend from their mountain hovels and offer fruits and vegetables for sale in the streets. They are, however, almost unsexed by their national ferocity and would not scruple to use their knives to any person who remarked that their charges were above those of the *Saddar Bazar* (Cantonment Market) of Peshawur. At the English cemetery here the band-master of an English regiment was found sleeping by a number of Afghans who at once carried him off but subsequently contrary to their practices, they sent him back uninjured.*
The fort of Jamrud was occupied by Hari Singh after a desperate battle which conferred such a halo of terror to his name that it is said the Afghan mothers even to this day employ that name to frighten their children to sleep.

---

* Morris's Guide to the Punjab.

Not far from this city in 1879 a battle was fought between the Indian and Afghan armies to the complete overthrow of the latter. Yakub Khan signed a treaty to the effect that the British Government should control the Khyber and Michni Passes and that a mission should be received in Cabul. The ambassador Sir Louis Cavagnari and his suite being sent in compliance with the treaty were accommodated in the Bala Hisar contiguous to the palace of the Ameer. Eventually a small knot of Afghan soldiers mutinied for their arrears of pay and attacked the residency, which was gallantly defended by the sepoys until all were killed, together with the embassy. The British expeditions, the one by the Khyber Pass and the other by the Korum Valley, were immediately undertaken for chastisement. At this time I made several applications for a post in Afghanistan but the result proving unsatisfactory I went to Babu Ram Chunder Mukherjee Head Assistant of the Commissariat Department Multan and personally represented my case saying if I could make a little money, I intended to continue my legal studies in England but I failed to obtain satisfaction as the gentleman considered I was too young to endure the perils of the field. Baffled in this attempt, I applied to Colonel Sibli at Ambala who held out hope and remembered his promise only after the termination of the war.

The remains of the Hindu and the Budhist temples between Peshawur and Cabul, and the Sanskrit names of the villages, as for instance, Penjdah (five villages) strongly impress me with the idea that caste-distinction was very little known to our Aryan forefathers. The restriction to travel over this country might advantageously be withdrawn, on condition that the Hindus of high caste, should keep to their Hindu diet, rice and lentils. It is incompatible with sound reason to assert that Indian diet impairs the health of a Hindu, or that English diet impairs the health of an Englishman, or that a cow should live on beef, and a tiger should thrive on grass. It is quite obvious that Nature has prescribed our food, dress, and other indispensable things, and it does not sound prudent on our part to act contrary to the rules of Nature by eating and

drinking that which is repugnant to the Hindu feeling.
In spite of our constant association with the English
people, in spite of our western civilization, we are not so
heartless as to ignore the feelings of our countrymen. But
whilst the humble Indian peasant is dying of famine,
with half-chewed grass in his mouth, no price appears
to some of my countrymen exorbitant to buy a ticket for
a *theatre*, to buy a bottle of champagne and other useless
things ; and on their arrival in India, they find that their
manners and customs, ideas and views are so alien to the
established principles of the Hindus, that the amalgamation of the parties is as impossible as the amalgamation of
oil and water. My case is entirely different. My income
is drawn not from India but from that country to which I
have the pleasure of rendering some service. I can
positively assure the world that I have never wasted even
a farthing in buying a ticket for a theatre or a bottle of
champagne, and several journals published in different
parts of the globe will guarantee my statement as perfectly
correct. The substance of one published in Madeira in
Africa, March 1886, is as follows :—

"The new *African Direct* who arrived at Madeira on the 7th of
February, under the ægis of Mr. Thomas, is a Hindu of high caste,
and is named Sasi Bhushan Sarbadhicary, and it is by the gracious
and readily granted permission of this gentleman that the present
Note finds itself in the columns of the *Monthly Correspondent.*

" Sasi, which means *moon*, is a *prænomen* (one can scarcely call it a
Christian name,) *Bhushan*, which signifies ornament, is a *cognomen*,
whilst Sarbadhicary, the correct signification of which is *possessor
of all things*, truly a proud title, is a family name, a special title
bestowed on an ancestor centuries ago, by a great potentate, as a
reward for a signal service to the state.

" Sarbadhicary belongs to the second of the four great Hindu
castes, which are the Brahmin, Kyasthu, Kshatria, Bhassa, but
although being of the second caste, his family by possessing the
title of Sarbadhicary is elevated to a rank superior to that of many
Brahmins

" Sarbadhicary was born in Bengal, but removed to the Punjab,
where he became a Member of the University College. He left
India for England at the age of nineteen, for the purpose of completing his studies. He entered Edinburgh University, where he
remained for some time, taking advantage of his vacations, for
making interesting and at the same time instructive tours through
all the countries on the continent excepting Russia, visiting with

special interest the old cities of classic Italy, the ancient edifices of which are now, alas, undergoing such ruthless treatment at the hands of modernizing " Philistines," would-be Hausmanns. Look for instance at Milan and Genoa. Sarbadhicary does not appear to have allowed one blade of the proverbial grass to grow under his feet, for whilst in Edinburgh, he took up amongst his other studies that of telegraphy, and since his arrival at Madeira, he has proved himself a very good sound reader. His favourite studies have been History and Law. He professes himself well acquainted with Roman and Scotch Law, and now he is about to tackle *English !* I wish him joy. I have seen his law books; the merest glance through their pages gave me a headache. Here during office hours his heart and soul are with his Recorder and Mirror signals, and he seems bent upon knowing everything all at once. The letters I have seen from Edinburgh professors could not be couched in more flattering terms, whilst letters from the Marquis of Ripon, Mrs. Gladstone, Mr John Bright and others, betoken a sincere and lively interest in his welfare. I have read a speech by our friend at Exeter Hall on the subject of *the abuse of early marriage in India*, in which social question he has taken a profound interest. As a proof that his sympathies in this direction are sincere, it suffices to say that ' for tenets he would not forsake he suffered pain, and ' if he did not ' court death ' he at least ran the gauntlet of exasperated relations and left Bengal rather than marry young, to the detriment of his studies, the expenses of which have always been defrayed by his own earnings. Here in Madeira our Hindu recruit spends the greater portion of his spare time in reading up and improving his mind. He does not, however, treat his body with the like amount of consideration or care, at least so it would appear, at first sight to the average Englishman; for no growing young Briton, Scot or Celt would thrive on rice for breakfast, rice and a little fish curry for dinner, and rice for " tea " with water *ad libitum*. The disappearance of a large water bottle, or rather its contents, at a meal draws many a sigh from the rascal Jose, who be it known supplied bottled Bass, &c., &c. Well after all Sasi (as we all call him for short) is quite right. Heavy English food would very likely damage *him* quite as much as rice and water every day would play old Harry with *me*."

" Whatever man has done, man may do " therefore, as I have thrived on rice, my countrymen can do so too.

I left Jamrud and reached Sukkur and Rohri Bunder *via* Multan. I spent but a short time in both the towns, which are separated by the Indus river. At the time of my visit a railway ferry crossed and re-crossed every now and then for the convenience of passengers ; but the sanction of the Government for building a bridge, had been obtained, and perhaps an useful structure now spans the Indus. From Sukkur a road runs to Sibi, where Mr. Alfred Perkins, the late Instructor of the Civil Training School, Bombay, has been transferred as a Telegraph Master; from the energy of his character, there is little doubt that under his guidance, the condition of the Telegraph Office has been considerably improved, but the former, I regret is sinking into oblivion. Mr. Perkins, with all his vivacity and invention, with all his multifarious knowledge, with his fluent speech and clear diction, can make the institution emerge from the eclipse with fresh splendour.

Sibi is in the valley of the Nari River which runs through the territory of the Khan of Khelat. It commands the entrance of the Bolan Pass. At no great distance is the Candahar State Railway where Bharu Mull, who worked under me as a signaller when in connection with the Indus Valley State Railway, has been employed as a Station Master. Bolan Pass is but 120 miles from Sibi; it is flanked by two high ranges of mountains and culminates in the plain *Dashti Bidalat* or Destitute Plain. The Pass is very narrow, sixty miles long and has two majestic hills about 8,500 feet high tapering to the clouds. Politicians and soldiers interested in the defence of our Indian Empire from aggression on the frontier should visit this pass, and see how Nature has provided for its defence : those who do so will return with the conviction that it is waste of money to regard Afghanistan as essential to the defence of India. Khandilani and Siribolan are very narrow passes which a score of well-trained soldiers could defend against overwhelming superiority of numbers. This is my own opinion, and I am glad to say an American soldier of distinction has confirmed it. There runs the Bolan River, which like others of mountainous origin, is rapid and frequently shifts its bed. In 1841 a detachment of British Troops was washed away. The Beluchis in the pass are professional robbers of relentless ferocity. I reached Kurrachee *viâ* Sukkur and Rohri, and went to the Telegraph Office, where I met two fellow signallers named Delastic, an Englishman, and Dusuiza, a Portuguese, who had worked with me in Bombay, for which place I eventually started.

Bombay has a fine harbour where scores of steamers belonging to various companies lay anchored. A strong stone wall protects the city from the encroachments of the sea, the waves of which strike the stone steps of the bathing quay with much violence and make such a great noise, as to suggest the idea that hundreds of crocodiles are engaged in one simultaneous conflict. It is said that the people even from the interior, go thither to take a sea-bath earnestly believing that a singular fate attends those who survive the effect of the immersion as sometimes they are borne away by the waves, sometimes lacerated by the sharks and devoured by crocodiles. The visitor to Bombay will find in its market amongst other local manufactures, silk of such gossamer delicacy, as is unknown even to the palace of Versailles or in the ball of St. James. In the course of his walk, he will see the muslins of Bengal, sabres of Oudh, jewels of Golconda, shawls of Cashmere, and filigree gold and silver work, ivory carvings, scarcely to be excelled in the world. This city in ancient time was subject to a Mahratta Chief. The Portuguese occupied it and granted it as a marriage-dowry to the Queen Infanta of Portugal. Bombay is a most beautiful city, on one side is the sea dotted with fleets laden with merchandize, on the other hills covered with date palm groves, the majestic palms, the supple banana, the crackling bamboo and the venerable mango and jack trees heavy with delicious fruits. On the breast of the sea stands Cape Elephanta which attests the antiquarian glory. Amidst such picturesque surroundings stands the Government telegraph office. Outside the compound is the nicely coloured terminal post, whence the wires are all skilfully led to the veranda and then to the battery room. There are about twenty-four wires which are almost as busy as the single wires of the main office of London. In the city there are four branch offices, the business excepting Mombadevie where I was, was slack. In the main office the signallers are of various creeds and colour, such as the English, Eurasians, Portuguese, Goanies, Hindus and Parsees. The Bombay Civil Training Institution furnished the best hands, but since the transference of Mr. Perkins Otukmund has assumed the best position.

CHAPTER V.

Marriage Rules and Social Rules—The Sufferings of the Widow Girl.

Whilst in Bombay, I received a note from a highly educated man named Cr. Sridhur of Lahore, recommending that before I left India for England, I should marry conditionally that the expenses of my education would be borne by the father of the bride and that if I signified my acceptance of this proposal, which was, as he said perfectly sound, the marriage could be legalized by a gentleman named Dutta Mahashaya* then residing in his house.

An English, Scotch or American will laugh at such a stipulation as he knows marriage is seldom undertaken in his country until after a considerable period of mutual acquaintance ; during which time the courting couple walk together, visit each other in their houses, and address each other in terms of affection. But the Indian marriage rule is entirely different. In the west, there are no inequalities of social position. Marriages can be celebrated as soon as an attachment proves mutual.

Our social rules are entirely different from those of the Western Countries. In India, no girl can be seen, as she

---

* Mahashaya means Sir. It is a title and is always placed after the name. Babu means Esquire, and is always placed before the name unlike Esquire which is placed after. Another peculiarity we have that in India when we show our respect to a party, we put on our caps, whereas in Western Countries, under similar circumstances, the people take off their hats. We enter a room with shoes off and caps on, and they enter with shoes on and hats off. Such is the characteristic difference which still exists.

is detained within the walls of her residence. The inside
is reserved for ladies and the outside for men. The meals
are cooked either by the ladies or by a professional cook
of priestly caste. Rice and fish are our chief food which
are distributed by the cook twice a day. In the West the
parties distribute themselves. Their stewards are detailed
to bring food and place it on tables. We do not eat on
tables. No knife or fork is provided for the Indians.
They sit on a square carpet a yard long and broad. The
cook serves rice on round brass plates. Dal or soup,
vegetables and currie are also provided. As soon as we
finish our meals, we wash our hands, and as soon as the
ladies finish theirs, they go to a pond, sometimes situated in
a garden attached to the building and purify themselves by
complete immersion. They pass and repass by a private
passage.

Rice is called Lakshmi (the goddess of wealth) but when
cooked its sanctity disappears to such an extent that if it
be merely touched by a foreigner or by a lower class of
Hindu, for instance a shoemaker or a carpenter, a higher
caste will have great objection to use it, should he do so,
he would be subject to excommunication.

My friends will think what a mysterious thing is caste
and will be curious to know something about it, but in a
small work like this, I cannot possibly advance and discuss
the subject in all its multifarious details; but I have
classified them as follows : -

Old begotted Hindus who are very good Sanskrit
scholars and have gone through philosophy, logic and
other branches of studies, think that they are the best people
on the face of the earth. The association of others would
prove ruinous to the growth of their religious as well as
social and moral welfare. Secluded as they are, their
knowledge dies with them.

A man named Wilson believing India a great place
for money, desired to share in it by some honest means.
On his arrival in Calcutta, he became a proprietor
of a Hotel. His methodical arrangement soon won
for him a great reputation and invited a large number
of Indians, who despite their caste, freely partook of the

food provided by Wilson   Now the question is whether the men are justified in violating the caste which has been suffered to exist from time immemorial.   Beef is most abhorrent to the Hindu population ; is it wise on the part of the fractional portion of such population to use it to the greatest annoyance of the Hindus ?   Supposing an Englishman inhabits a region where monkey-meat is considered the food of highest flavour, having partaken of it, will he continue to do so even on his return to his native country, I reply negatively.   Personally, I can only say, it would be a matter of great regret had I been induced to partake of beef or other food repugnant to the usages of my countrymen ; but my feeling in this matter always protected me from such an offence.   I am entitled to call this class Wilson's Hindus.   The other class is called *quasi* English ; as they are neither Indians nor English. In dress and food they are English, in colour they are like the Indians, and in education they are neither.

The evening meal also is served in the same way, the men claiming prior opportunity to feed themselves and leave the residue for the ladies.   The migration of the ladies having been strictly confined from their house to the tank and *vice versa*, no males can see them.   Accordingly a class named Ghatack is appointed to select suitable boys and girls for marriage.   His duty is the observation of young people to ascertain to what class they belong, whether either of the parties is of noble family, mukha, or chief, if so, then what number.   The education of the bridegroom is tested by the father of the bride.

It had never been my intention to marry and settle in India, but I would have acceded in consideration that my pecuniary difficulty would be removed, had not the same social custom forced me to postpone the idea until I finished my studies in the Western countries.

It is an all-pervading rule that on the death of the husband the young wife, no matter what her age, has to subsist on one meal, consisting of rice and vegetables, daily.   On special fast days, named Akadashi, she is not allowed food at all, and in every month there are two such unfortunate Akadashis, which, owing to the extreme youth of many of the Indian widows, is severely trying to immature constitutions. I feared if I died whilst in the pursuit of my studies in the Western countries, my wife would submit herself to all the hardships of the social custom. It seems not a little selfish that the men should thus reserve feasting days for themselves, allowing the fasting ones to devolve on the weaker sex. This is but the minutest fractional part of the sadness of her life.

As soon as the death is announced to the family the members weep bitterly and loudly, when, according to the customary law, some lady, who must be a member of the bereaved family, as none of other family should interfere with her as she has been subject to what Roman law calls *capitis diminutio* on account of the death, takes the left hand of the girl and knocks off the ornament called Louha which is made of gold or silver and which is the sure prognostic of the existence of the husband, she subsequently removes the vermillion from the forehead of the girl. The absence of these two signs indicates the death of her husband. Forthwith the rest of her ornaments are taken off. At length her nice linen cloth, called Sari worn by married girls is removed and a coarse linen is substituted.

This is but the commencement of the indignities to which her bereavements subject her. She is now universally hated as Randi, or husbandless girl. She is no longer permitted the companionship of girls of similar age. They believe, if they kept company with this unfortunate one, they might share her fate. Ao (the girls with husbands) will not condescend even to speak to her. She can only relieve her monotony by the company of widows like herself, but according to the Hindu proverb, Bedar barra bamanar chuta (the youngest member of the highest caste and the eldest member of the lowest are destined to serve), this girl is constrained to work hard to satisfy the elder widows and the slightest disobedience is reported to the domineering mother-in-law.

It is maintained there are three classes of men and women Deb (godly) Rakshashas (cannibal) and Nara (men). A deb girl can be united in marriage to either of these classes, but if the cannibal girl is united to a Nara boy and if he meets his fate, which is quite possible, the death is attributed to the result of the unfortunate union. Such is the type of many of the superstitions which prevail in our community. But God, our Almighty Father, is the arbiter of our destinies. None can interfere with His decree.

The mother-in-law on a report subjects her to such severe ill-treatment, that the very name Shashoory (mother-in-law), inspires in her the greatest terror. Instances are not rare in which the mistress has employed her cane, in severe chastisement on this unfortunate girl. The young widow is precluded by social law from going out and speaking to anybody of the opposite sex.

Although debarred from any sympathy, she works much harder than even a maid-servant would be willing to do. Under such dismal surroundings, she avails herself of every leisure moment and withdraws to a lonely room, to relieve herself by weeping, but at every footstep, she hurriedly wipes away her tears and resumes the domestic work assigned to her, as she dreads the approach of her mother-in-law who is sure to punish her for exhibition of useless sorrow (as she calls it) and negligence to her work.

However, thank God, that her mental distress is not without remedy. She can expect considerable solace and sympathy from her parents, provided they are wealthy. Since they occasionally relieve the monotony of her life, by inviting her to their house by means of an Indian palankeen carried by four robust coolies. It is covered up on all sides. It has two handles which are placed on the shoulders of the bearers.

On the arrival at her parents' house, she represents all the malpractices to which she had been subject in her mother-in-law's house. Indeed no maid-servant is constrained to perform half as much work nor does she bear half as much chastisement ; because she knows, that she is a working woman and that wherever she works, her rice and salt will be provided.

The cruelties perpetrated during antique period by the task masters towards the Israelites of Egypt, that which was practiced by the Patricians towards the Plebeians, during the glorious days of the Roman Empire, that which was practiced by the Americans, towards their African slaves before they were emancipated in 1861-1864, were merciful and humane in comparison with the cruelty to which the unfortunate widow girls are exposed, not for a day or so, not for months, but as long as their lives last. It is owing to this reason and some other reasons that I condemn early marriage.

In the 19th century when civilization is far advanced, the task masters do not exist to tyrannize over the unfortunate descendants of Jacob ; long before the fall of the Roman Empire, the race-distinction in Rome was so far super- seded as to enable the masters and slaves to meet on a common platform, and to discuss all social and political questions and bind themselves by an indissoluble fraternal tie. Abraham Lincoln, the great Champion of Christian Faith, honestly believing the existence of slavery would be injurious to the prosperity and the growth of the American nation, sealed the manumission by his noble blood.

In the West, social and domestic cruelty is exposed to public criticism both by the press and on the platform. But in India such a thing is impossible, the ladies being secluded, their domineering influence is confined to their hearth which is never resorted to by any male.

One day in July 1889, whilst working in the main office Western Union Company Syracuse I went to seek a comfortable boarding house, accompanied by the Assistant Secretary of the Young Men's Association. He knocked at the door of a house situated in his neighbourhood. A young lady opened it and being informed about our mission, admitted us. The landlady being absent, she herself assigned to me one of the most comfortable rooms. My residence in the house, apprised me that the condition of the girl was far from enviable ; as her husband in the heat of liquor, I understood, exposed the innocent one, to most cruel indignities. I further learned that he was out of employment for some time and the wife had to work in an office the whole day long, with a view to support her husband and her baby. On returning home at night, she had to cook for her husband and for the

D

baby. The former under pretence of illness never applied to anybody for work but was entirely dependent on the income of his wife. At morning she arose, prepared breakfast, for the two (as she herself took her meals in her office) and went to her business. The man arose and took his breakfast and went to bed again. He arose for the second time in an advanced hour of the day and placed the baby on a perambulator and went out for a walk. At night they met in the house and the husband began to chastise and ill-use his wife. This happened almost every day. Once I left the office at a late hour of night and reached home only three hundred yards distant. I was received by the lady with her usual vivacity and courtesy, but thete ars trickling down her cheeks, too plainly revealed, the malpractices to which she had been subjected by her husband. With a view to draw him from the company of his wife, I told him " an electric light had just been set up in the neighbourhood and that it was producing such dazzling effect as to deserve special attention." As soon as we were on the high road, I interceded on behalf of the wife, requesting him to desist from any vicious practice and to try to arrive at an amicable settlement, representing how she had satisfied him by the faithful and assiduous discharge of domestic duties, and with what regards she had re-plenished him with money. Her faithful service and devotion should bind him by a tie of gratitude, in remembrance of which he should always respect and appreciate her quality, and that in case Providence dooms her to a sudden death his repentance for the loss of such a wife would be very great.

I was extremely glad to learn that my words were n ot without effect as since then, their disagreement sank into oblivion and the man gradually became more amiable to his wife.

Now in this case the difficulty in restoring harmony to this couple, was lessened by the representation of a few adequate words which would have been quite im-possible in similar case in India; as I have already related that the Indian ladies could not be seen and none knows what happens in the high walls of female department.

There is no prescribed time for marriage. The parents think it is ·their duty to effect it as early as possible, and when the matrimonial tie has been consummated, they think they have done remarkably well, without giving any attention whatever to the future happiness of the parties. The outcome of their work has the following disastrous effect. We have at present 24,000 widowers and 78,000 widows between six and nine years of age; 75,000 widowers and 207,000 widows between ten and fourteen years of age, 131,000 widowers 382,000 widows between sixteen and nineteen years of age. Almost all the widows are subject to the same ill-usage as has been already described. I am indebted to my statistics in this matter to Surgeon-General Balfour.

To such a monstrous evil, no other remedy could be conveniently applied, than the stoppage of early marriage. We feel greatly indebted to Pundit Ishwar Chunder Bidbasagor, for his most valuable work. " Widow Marriage." The amplitude and fertility of his intellect, his great literary talent for controversy and social and administrative faculty, combined with his undaunted moral courage and fervent zeal for the welfare and prosperity of India, entitle him to our best praise.

Legislative measures which would restrict marriage to the minimum age of twenty for men and fourteen for girls would, in my opinion, remove this terrible state, of affairs, though undoubtedly my idea would encounter considerable opposition from bigotted Hindus.

A boy can marry as often as he likes. He can marry one; on her death, he can marry a second; and on her death a third and so on, but if he likes he can marry a number of them successively though all may be alive; but widow marriage is very rare. I am acquainted with a gentleman in Patna, who has forty-nine wives. He has no house; nor does he do any work but he has a note-book wherein he has carefully written the names and addresthe of all his wives and those of their parents, to whom ses gentleman is an object of great love and respect. When he visits them, he is most cordially received and hospitably entertained. Unfortunately his stay in each house could be but of limited duration as there are 52 weeks in a year, for the performance of his 49 visits. The death of such a polygamist, which makes all his wives widows, is most bitterly regretted. Hence the number of widows greatly exceeds that of widowers.

A lower-class girl, comparatively speaking, enjoys more liberty than the higher one, as the former can go wherever she pleases. If widowed, she is entitled to re-marry. In the absence of such re-marriage she is not restricted to one meal a day. She need not observe the rules of fasting. If disinclined to work, she can retire into a garden and enjoy the fruits of the trees which nature has so plentifully lavished on this favoured land, as are unknown to any other part of the globe.

There are two classes of marriage, *Gharjamya* and ordinary. The former is prevalent among wealthy people who give their daughter in marriage to such a bridegroom who is a boy of plain good sense, having no desire to be a university man, an author or a debater, but if he can read and write he is amply satisfied. His father is the *mukha* or the chief, who holds the thread of caste, and is universally respected. No matter whether he has any money or not, the princes and landlords are very glad to receive him most cordially and always gratefully remunerate him if he visits them in their houses on a day of marriage or some other festivity. He is the *pater-familias* of his house all his sons and daughters and wives (always more than one), and grandchildren, maid-servants, and men servants are under his *potestas*. According to Roman law his death, makes all his children *sui juris*, but according to Hindu law his *persona* descends to his eldest son, or, in other words, the status of a British lord descends to his eldest son, who has the same rights, duties and corresponding position as his father had. The younger sons are called lords out of courtesy. Similarly according to Hindu social law, the *persona* descends to the eldest, provided he is not subject to any *capitis deminutio*, by doing something contrary to Hindu law, then he assumes his father's *caput* and all the rest of the members of his family are to the eye of Hindu law as much *filius familias* -under the care of the new man as they were during the time of his father. But all are invested with the dignities *janma-mukhi* (born chief), or *bera-mukhi* (increased chief). Thus to a certain extent the family resembles the Roman and to a certain extent, it resembles the British lord's family. The younger brothers can represent their eldest brother in some public meetings and will be received as cordially and will be as much remunerated as their elder brother.

According to Roman law, the death of the paterfamilias makes his children *sui juris* at once, but according to Indian law it is entirely different. As soon as the eldest boy arrives at the age of twelve, his father proposes that he should be married to a daughter of a *mukha* (chief). She must be the eldest daughter of her father. If her number is twenty-six (which number now-a-days has become obsolete) the boy must be the same, otherwise there is no marriage. If the age of the girl be one year, nay six months or one month, lame or blind, that does not invalidate the marriage. If she be very ugly still the marriage could be completed. But the price of the girl is most exorbitant. Despite all the defects, the father of the bridegroom will receive the girl, with great joy provided he can meet the charge. The father of the girl most probably being the man of the highest caste does not do any work but lives on the income of the sale of his daughter, so he expects an enormous sum of money for this girl; the other party is quite unable to pay the price, which sometimes amounts to £400 to £500 including ornaments. People who are not conversant with our custom will disbelieve my statement, saying it is improbable ; but they do not know that the main object of the marriage is to secure the head of the family from loss of caste. At the present moment there are men who are quite willing to pay more than the above sum, provided they get a girl number twenty-six which cannot be had.

To say briefly, as soon as the marriage is complete, the position of the father of the boy is most conspicuous. Then the boy is again united to the daughter of a prince, whose caste is not very high but whose wealth is great.   The boy gets a palace with servant, garden, carriage and horse. Instances of this are not rare.   The prince is willing to give his daughter to this boy because soon after the death of his father he will be the chief and his son will be invested with the double title, the prince on one side and the chief on the other.   The glory of the father is not ended here if he has some more sons as it is now unnecessary to pay any money, his caste being well secured, he will get at least £150 in cash and ornaments and other things; and if he has a daughter then his position is still higher, as he will get for her the same amount as he has himself paid.   But the price of the second daughter is not much as she cannot secure the title chief on behalf of her husband she can make him only *Kanistha* or assistant chief.   The only son of a chief is forced to marry a number of girls as his first marriage reduces him to poverty, and he wants to ameliorate his condition by wealthy marriages. The first marriage which is very dearly effected is called ordinary and the second is *gharjamaya* in which the son enjoys the rich *dos* which under no circumstances could be alienated by the husband and is reserved for the wife, who being under the *potestas* of the members of her family cannot interfere with the state consequently she simply enjoys the *usufructus*.   Her son when he arrives at maturity can do what he pleases with the property.

Another object which forces early marriage is religion. The enjoyment of dowry and other things are rather the accessory motives of marriage.   Punnama Narakat tryata ja sha putra.   (That person is the son who saves his father from falling into hell).   The son attends the funeral ceremony which is different from that of other parts of the globe.

CHAPTER VI.

The Ghost story—The funeral—The abolition of the Suttee—My participation in a funeral.

When the owner of a house is dangerously ill, he is attended and served in the same way as the people of other parts of the globe under similar circumstances. On the approach of his dissolution, he is removed to the sacred banks of the Ganges, where death has a most significant effect, as the deceased is thereby transferred to heaven but if he suffers to die in the house, he becomes a ghost and hovers about the neighbourhood.

It is a proof of the strong belief in supernatural reappearance that when an Indian dies, the people are more afraid of the corpse, than of tigers and leopards. Ladies and children leave the locality and the persons. who are to handle the dead body sometimes are equally feared. They are not allowed to return to their residence without an ablution in the sacred river, in the absence of that particular river the Ganges any other would be preferable. It is a source of trouble on the part of that individual whose relative or parents are dead. The difficulty arises from the fact that he is constrained to perform most of the works almost single-handed. Specially so if his means are limited. Very few will be disposed to furnish him any useful aid. So the greatest difficulty of a Hindu is that which arises from the death of a relative. Occa-. sionally it has been observed that dead bodies have been carried away through villages almost desolate.

In a village named Valuka there is a tank named Baman

Khali. It is affirmed that on one occasion a priest, being
very thirsty, descended into it to drink water. He was
caught by a ghost who killed him, hence it obtained the
name "Baman Khali." It has now been appropriated for
burning dead bodies only. Above the tank there is a fine
building situated in a fine orchard, where an Englishman
resided. It is rumoured that one night a ghostly visitant
entered his room and disturbed him whilst sleeping. He
arose, loaded his gun and fired, upon which the intruder
laughed and vanished into the air. He subsequently retired
to a factory five miles distant until his return to England.

Another story runs thus :—On a stormy and rainy night,
some people from a fair which happens once a week in the
aforesaid village, took shelter in the building to pass that
night only as they could not get a shelter anywhere else,
the number of the houseless people being more numerous
than the villagers could accommodate. A tremendous
voice frightened them almost to death and they had to
leave their temporary residence in spite of the rain and
thunder-storm. Some students having talked about this,
provoked one of their bold comrades, who never believed
in the existence of ghosts. The student who related this
story promised to pay five rupees to any individual who
could go to a shashan,* and hammer a peg down as an
indication that the party had fulfilled his mission. Thereupon the man hesitatingly undertook the task of hammer-
ing it in a prescribed shashan. The youth with trembling
steps reached the spot and accomplished the object.
Fearing the approach of a ghost, he attempted to run
away but he could not succeed as some one appeared to
be pulling him from behind ; he had heard people say
that a ghost pulls a person by his dress, and that he subsequently kills the man. Having been subject to such
terror he soon expired. The explanation of this tragic
death could be given thus :—The natives of Bengal wear
a thin white linen about five yards long one yard broad
hanging from the waist to their feet. The youth had
heedlessly hammered the peg through his linen and thus

* A place where dead bodies are burnt.

shackled himself to the spot. When attempting to run away the pull of his pinned linen (to the ground) was attributed to that of the ghost and thus he died of mere terror.

I remember during my boyhood, I visited this tank, I swam in it and picked the nice water lilies. I climbed the pear tree and the dwarf orange tree situated in the orchard, without provoking the reputed ghostly residents.

The moribund is removed to a lonely cottage, situated on the bank of the Ganges. The bearers belong to the same caste with the patient as the priests would not condescend to carry him nor would he submit to the idea of being carried by inferior class of people. In that desolate place they are forced to spend many a sleepless night with the dying. They cook their own meals and sleep on the bare ground. When rain falls no matter with what violence, they are forced to expose themselves to it, as they cannot leave the patient unprotected. Sometimes he lives long and becomes troublesome, and sometimes he is restored to health and returns home, but generally he perishes.

Soon after his death he is placed on a pile of wood to which fire is set. Formerly it was the universal practice that the widow of the deceased volunteered to be burnt, with the corpse as a heroic Suttee. Prince Ram Mohun Rai visited Lord William Bentinck, the then Governor-General, and strongly represented the opinion of the enlightened Hindus, that such a horrible practice should be suppressed. Although the British Government had solemnly averred, that they would never interfere with the religious and social customs of the Indian people, Lord Bentinck abolished the Suttee, in spite of the opposition of the priests and other Hindus. Nor are we legitimately entitled to blame the Government for abrogating the cruel practice, as the rulers would respect only those customs which do not encroach upon the claims of humanity, personal freedom and the rights of property.

Another chivalrous Bentinck is necessary to stop the the system of early marriage, so that girls under ten years of age may not be subject to the cruelty perpetuated by the mother-in-law. The noble Lord has ameliorated the evil but to his successors is left the duty of abolishing the entire malpractice.

Resuming the description of the disposal of the dead I
beg to say, the corpse when reduced to ashes, the
cinerary remains are washed away in the sacred water
of the Ganges and the men plunge and purify themselves.

During my boyhood at Valuka, I undertook the office of
carrying the corpse of a lady, belonging to the same caste as
myself. Four of us succeeded in conveying it to the
desolate part of the sacred river, but the total absence of
wood in that locality precluded the possibility of our
burning it, so we picked up an earthen vessel and filled it
with the river sand and attached it to the corpse as a
weight and plunged it into the deep water. In the Western
Countries there are a select number of people who are
denominated "undertakers," whose business is to undertake
the responsibility of giving to the corpse an honourable
burial. In India there is a class of people called Mudda
Faras the member of which wears a dirty linen, a
yard long and six inches broad round his waist; the rest
of his body is as naked as he was when his mother brought
him on earth. He is never afraid of a ghost as he
himself, I believe, is one of the members of this class, at
least his long hair and beard, his black complexion generate
equal fear. He could be hired only in cities and towns.
No higher class person condescends to accept this office.
although we have on our record that similar service had
been performed by King Harish Chunder, when reduced
to poverty. His wife in disguise entered the service of a
gentleman, with her only boy six years old. After three
years the boy died, and the corpse remained in the house
for several hours, contrary to Hindu law. None assisted
the queen to remove the corpse. At length at 1 a.m.
when all asleep she herself quietly conveyed it to the place
where the king was an undertaker. The husband and the
wife could not recognise each other, but the former refused
funeral at that unreasonable hour whereupon being greatly
disappointed, she fell flat and wept bitterly saying "The
fate has its way." Ill fated as she was, the all-surveying
Providence has pulled her down from a dizzy height.
Then the king recognised his wife and they sympathized
with each other in their mutual misfortunes. They were

subsequently restored. The Bible tells us " Do not hate any condition lest it happen to be thy own."

Prior to our return home, we had another function to perform, as immersion in the sacred river, after participation in such duties is enforced by our religious customs. But the difficulty to achieve this object was almost insurmountable. The bank was steep and a crocodile was floating on the surface of the water, consequently it was hazardous to risk a bathing.. It is said as soon as the animal sees a victim, it sinks out of sight. In an instant it re-appears exactly on the same spot, catches the victim and carries it off before any aid can avail. The only remedy a man can employ under such dismal circumstances is to sit down on the neck of the animal and thrust simultaneously both his forefingers into its eyes, which are said to be most vulnerable. Then it rushes towards the bank and upon ridding itself of its rider, plunges again into the water. As soon as the man, who has undergone such a perilous ride, is thrown on dry land, the herdsmen, who work in the fields, promptly run to his assistance and remove him from the path of further danger. I have got this information from two different persons who were themselves caught and narrowly escaped death by the same means as described. During June and July when the rivers overflow their banks, a milkmaid* was crossing a road where there were about two feet deep Ganges water. She was carried off. The whole of her body was lacerated ; she saved herself by the presence of mind. A student in Calcutta related that he went to drink water into the shallow part of a river† he was caught and saved himself by the same process.

Under such circumstances, thinking it would be mere waste of time to deliberate, I jumped into the water and

---

* A milkmaid is a lower class girl, so she is permitted to walk in any thoroughfare.

† We drink river-water whereas it is very seldom employed in Europe and in America. When we are thirsty we drink water in which drink India still has ascendency over the Western Countries. but I fear she will not retain it long, as all her principal towns Calcutta,. Bombay and Madras have been crowded with drunkards.

plunged my body twice (only one plunge is necessary on the death of a relative) and returned to the bank. My example was followed by one of my comrades but the two remaining returned home after an immersion in a tank, and were regarded as very irreligious.

From the moment of the death, all the religious rites of the family are suspended for eleven days, if the party is of priestly caste ; otherwise for a month. The man who washes clothes will decline theirs. The barber will decline to shave them. The men should walk barefooted and bare-headed through the streets. A woman never uses shoes but always stays in barefooted. She might be the richest person in the world still she submissively conforms to the social rule of walking in-door barefooted. They restrict themselves to one meal a day. After the prescribed time a propitious day arrives, when the barber about 1 p.m., shaves them because he shaves others first and this family last, and when purified by an immersion his offence of shaving the bereaved family is forgiven.

When shaving followed by an immersion is over, a great customary banquet is held, with occasionally a gigantic proportion of magnificence which necessitates the most lavish outlay ; and it is affirmed that the one given by Prince Nobokissen, on the death of his mother, cost him £6,000,000 sterling. The people generally spend money in proportion to their means and those who do so are ultimately reinstated.

The children worship family idols and give funeral cakes to the deceased, but in the entire absence of children, the father is supposed to go to hell, so the marriage is based on this superstition. Another motive which induces parents to encourage early marriage is to enable their children to lead virtuous lives. Immorality is visited with severe punishment and frequently both the wrong-doer and the wronged are excommunicated from society. Such ostracised persons are never re-admitted into the family. Their relatives close their doors against them. Food, nay even a glass of water is denied to them. Virtually we lose more by early marriage than we gain ; I have observed instances in which a married youth has led an immoral life whereas an unmarried one has led a most virtuous life ; as the latter most probably being attached to some favourite branch of studies, pays very little attention to any criminal objects.

———————————————

CHAPTER VII.

The Indian priests—The Hindu religion—The description of King Vicramaditta—My difficulty from leopards—The description of Nrishinga—The description of Hiranna Kashupa.

An Indian priest is generally a proficient Sanskrit scholar. His text is the original Sanskrit work written on palm leaves. He carries it wherever he goes and reads out a passage, not to the audience but to the domestic gods for worshipping whom he travels from one house to another. According to the Western custom, the parson goes to his church and reads a passage out of the Bible to the audience and delivers an address upon the application of the passage which he selects as the text. Thus the ways in which the priests of two different religions impart their religious truths to the disciples are so widely diverging as never to agree. The priests of Nuddea, a place which stands almost on the same platform with Benares, are very highly educated people. The noteworthy priest or pundit (learned man) has a religious institution or tole, where he admits a number of poor students and imparts education free of charge. He also feeds them and defrays the expense out of his own pocket, in recompense of which the student volunteers to pay a certain fee called Dakshina, at the completion of his studies. But he exempts an indigent student from the payment of Dakshina. The pundit is indeed so profound a scholar that I was forced to say to Dr. Peck, Professor of the Columbia College, New York, "the best Sanskrit authority of Europe and America will prove unequal to him." Once, one of his favourite (indigent) students, on completing his studies, applied to the pundit who is called guru or teacher to accept some Dakshina. It is maintained in the absence of some payment to the guru, the education of a man (the women are not allowed to study) is very seldom complete. On refusal he persisted and thereby provoked the teacher who imposed such an enormous charge upon the distressed student that he could not pay. The legend tells us he prostrated before the image of Siva (Supreme Deity) who recommended him to Kuvera, the god of wealth, who replenished the student with such an inexhaustible supply of money, as to exceed the amount, the guru demanded. Whatever be the case the noble institution which the latter keeps, deserves the highest encomium of all philanthropists.

Nuddea is a great religious seat having the shrines of all gods and goddesses. Durga, Roma and Kali have been most prominently represented. On a great festive day called Potpurnima large images from twenty to thirty feet high are made of straw and worshipped. I visited this place once and was very kindly entertained. The hospitality in this city is proverbial. Wherever a person goes, he is received kindly and amply supplied with prasad (the remnant of the meal eaten by God). The guest is assured of a comfortable resting place to sleep at night. Anything in the shape of payment or gratuity is declined. The object, of extending this open-handed hospitality to the people without being informed anything about their antecedents, is that they are the children of God and to satisfy the requirements of the children would be to propitiate the All-Father Who will reward the host in the next generation,* with higher status than he enjoys in this.

It is said that Prince Vicramaditta inquired of his chief pundit Kalidasa " who was he in the past and what made him King of the Universe in the present generation." Believing he would not be able to solve the difficult problem, he returned home and quietly went to bed, instructing his

---

* It is maintained that we are re-born on the earth soon after we die. Whosoever has rendered good office will have a noble birth and whosoever has done contrary will have an ignoble one after his death.

servants under no circumstances should he be disturbed.
But his only little daughter seeing her father had lost his
wonted vivacity, knocked at his door and asked him to take
his usual meal, and that she would endeavour to relieve him
of his trouble. The father pleased with the encouraging
words took his customary meal and went to the court.
Now he was the head pundit; a man of recognised merit
and a great scholar so his reputation would have been
greatly depreciated had he not succeeded in giving a satisfactory reply. Whatever the educated father failed to do
was accomplished by the able daughter.

It is commonly believed that after the death of a man,
he is summoned before the Great Magistrate (God) and is
tried. The dead is then re-born in mundane families
good or bad according to the merits and demerits of his
previous life. If a man has been philanthropic and has
improved the value of his life by the establishment of
institutions to impart education to destitute children, if he
has succored the distressed by giving food to the starved,
clothes to the ragged, and worshipped gods and goddesses, then, on his death, he attends the court of the
Deity who instructs him to take his birth in the highest
caste who are happy, wealthy and comfortable. As
soon as he is re-born, he forgets all about his past
generation and performs the work of this present one. If
he does the same glorious actions with which he signalized
his past, he is blessed with even better reward; but if he
be guilty of a crime, he renews his birth under circumstances of degradation proportionate to his vices. This
belief induces even a bad and reckless man to think about
futurity remembering on the judgment day, he will suffer
or reap the fruit of his iniquity by the circumstances of his
subsequent existence. Nor is it known whether on his
return to the earth, his birth will be confined to the human
family or to the most degraded of the animal species. I
have heard people say in the present generation they
suffer from the consequence of their past existence, in case
they are negligent to fulfil their duties in this, they will
suffer more in the next. So they show hospitality and
other virtues gladly and willingly.

We learn from the girl that King Vicramaditta was a poor man having a wife, who had borne him five boys and a girl. His name was Shantanu who subsisted entirely by his manual labor. His exertions barely sufficed to support such a large family. So he was forced to live only on one meal a day. Once a hungry Brahmin visited him and implored relief. The owner had neither money nor food to satisfy the necessity of the stranger. But the hospitable entertainment of the guest whom God sends is a sacred office, the performance of which could never be refused by such a pious man as Shantanu. Accordingly he invited him to dinner which was ready and was divided into eight parts, two for the husband and wife and the rest for the children. The customary rule in India is that the guest is fed first. So Shantanu gave him his part which did not appease his hunger, then at the request of her husband, the wife gladly gave hers, but the traveller wanted more. The children successively gave theirs with every mark of anger and contempt, with an unkind remark that " whilst the beggar father could not support his own family and children, he invited a stranger." The man consumed all and departed. This was related in the full court of the King, who himself listened with great attention and in credulity. He wanted some proofs for the substantiation of this statement. But he was asked to desist as it is the universal belief among the Hindus, that a person meets his fate, as soon as he becomes cognisant of the circumstances of his previous existence. The King persisted. So Kalidasa communicated his dilemma to his little daughter, who forthwith repaired to the palace in a palankeen. A screen divided the pasture allotted to the gentlemen, from that where the girl was surrounded by the ladies of the King's household. She ordered for the five oxen of a grocer, and a cow of a sweeper. On their arrival the girl said they were his children, upon which some of them dropped dead. They were thus degraded in this generation because in the preceding one, when their father asked for their shares of food, they gave grudgingly and with contemptuous

E

remarks. The King further sought to be informed of the condition of his wife, whereupon he was requested to desist and not to risk greater harm and misfortune. But the King was inexorable, so the girl returned to her mother who was anxiously awaiting some cordial news of the proceedings at the court. The daughter, with a heavy heart, represented it was the will of Heaven that she should die and that her duty consisted in trustful resignation and submission to God's will. Having taken an affectionate farewell of her mother and the rest of the family, she returned to the court and informed the King that she herself was the wife and immediately died, to the greatest regret of the vast concourse of people. Having learned that to the virtuous action of his previous existence, he was indebted for the kingdom over which he then ruled, he displayed even greater philanthropy, justice and generosity than before. He continued to lead a most simple life. The furniture of his sitting-room consisted of a mat and an earthen vessel of cold water. His reputation was universal. His court was visited by the *literati* and men of genius from afar. Kalidasa the Indian Shakespeare, and Bhababhuti the Indian Milton were his trustworthy courtiers.

The priests of Bengal appreciative of the blessings which God has bountifully showered upon them, seek by the practice of virtue and hospitality to deserve in the next generation still greater favor at His hand. They seldom refuse shelter or refreshment; but as the guests are admitted without any previous knowledge of them, their hospitality is open to abuse from the ungrateful and dishonest.

When about twelve years of age, I attended a school at Kishnaghur, but spent the holidays generally at my residence Valuka, about six miles distant from the place of my studies. During the winter months I went home on Saturday, spent the night and Sunday. On Monday morning I attended the school at 10 a.m. This arrangement was impracticable during summer, for the heat being very great, the school commenced at 6 a.m. and closed at 10 a.m. So in the warm season I went home on

Saturday evening, but unless I left on Sunday and spent the night at Kishnaghur (in the house either of Babus Banku Behary Khan or Ram Chunder Mukherjee, who very graciously sheltered me beneath their hospitable roofs), I could not possibly attend the school at morning.

One evening when I had lingered at Valuka until after sunset, I started on this journey, walking fast and running at intervals, for the weather was cloudy and stormy when in the semi-darkness the warning-cry " fao," of a fox* which has so often proved serviceable to the belated traveller, announced that a leopard was lurking in the neighbourhood. Unfortunately I had nothing with me useful as a defensive weapon save an umbrella, and although I was aware that there was a small village in the vicinity, the darkness of the night obscured the track. I did not lose the presence of mind, remembering a well-known and often-quoted Sanskrit passage, which says "Don't be afraid, when the object of apprehension is at hand, but take every precaution to remedy it." I hastened towards the village with redoubled exertion, and reached the house belonging to a man of priestly caste, who very kindly entertained me, with board and lodge free of charge. The next morning I expressed my gratitude, and went to the school. I was often almost in the grasp of the ferocious animal, but the merciful Providence protected me from harm.

Once I was travelling by a bullock train from Kishnaghur to Valuka, when the conveyance arrived at the village which is situated between the two, some women warned the drivers of two conveyances, to be careful, as they had seen some ferocious animal, but as they did not mention its name, the drivers took very little notice. Hardly had we gone three hundred yards further, a leopard was found lying beneath a thicket facing us. The driver of the first carriage said to the other, on whose carriage I was, " Have you seen?" The latter was afraid to reply lest the former should point him out with his forefinger, which is such a signal insult, that leopards are said to revenge even

* The fox invariably notifies the presence of a tiger, leopard or wolf by this cry; but should the latter run after him, he changes the cry to " fac " " fac."

E 2

at a most imminent risk. It was just twilight which in India lasts only a few minutes ; although the animal never attempted to dispute our passage, I was rather afraid and much more so when the carriage left me alone, for they were bound for another village. The darkness and the fear of the animal persuaded me to seek a shelter at the first village I arrived at. I went to a Mahommedan, as the village was inhabited only by this class, who very kindly received me but being a member of a higher caste, I could not partake of his meal, so the owner requested me to cook my own, assuring, every necessary arrangement would he made to accomplish this object, to which proposal I reluctantly acceded.

On another occasion in the same neighbourhood, I was riding a horse, sent to me by a friend of mine named Mr. Bipra Dass Pall Choudry. I informed the groom who was with me, that the locality possessed a notorious character, and related to him an incident, in which a gentleman was passing through the field, (it was actually a large field) in a bullock train, when a leopard disputed his passage, by sitting down on the road. The two oxen shook off their yoke, and ran away in terror. Although strongly fortified inside the train, he was about to faint. The conspicuous courage displayed by his driver could hardly be exaggerated. Armed only with his whip he descended, cried loudly and noisily struck the whip on the yoke, to frighten the adversary, who thereupon withdrew ayard and sat again ; the man occupied the vacant space, by drawing his cart forward and repeated the same process ; and thus for over two hours the one advanced and the other retreated. After so manœuvring for that time, his cries were heard by a number of villagers, who armed with staves, drove the mighty antagonist. I requested the groom, should we meet any beast of prey, not to run away but to unite our strength and repel the foe. The man replied "I fear you will run away leaving me in the grasp of the animal." I said "I pledge my word that I will never do any such thing," upon which he was satisfied and conformed to my request. We soon reached another village, where some people whom I never saw before, asked me to spend the night with them. But in the aforesaid cases I was alone, whereas now I had some one to help me, so I refused their kind offer with thanks.

The name of the village where people so often meet the animal is Dehpara. It consists of two words Day and Para. The former is the corruption of Deb, which means God and Para means a village, God's village. The name has the following origin. In antiquity a milkman, who resided in that neighhourhood, had a very fine cow which furnished many quarts of milk every day, except that when she entered a very particularly thick jungle. One day the owner followed his cow, which began to graze in an open space, almost surrounded by impervious jungle. He saw the god Nrishingha, who arose from the earth, and began to drink the milk. The man ashamed of his watch, fell prostrate and implored forgiveness. The god pardoned him and informed the prince of Kishnaghur, in a dream that he desired to live on earth. The prince promised the erection of a magnificent building and that pundits, thoroughly conversant with all the various systems of worship and prayer, would be employed to wait upon him. But the god replied a small resting place would suffice. Accordingly the jungle was cleared, a small building erected, the priests appointed and a tank dug. The dignity and sanctity of this god is universally acknowledged as very great, and people, from the remotest parts of India, visit the sacred place to solicit his favors. The persons without family, and those without children apply for the gratification of their desire, and when their applications are granted they give grand feasts. A person whose son is dangerously ill beseeches him for his recovery. The marriage of the daughter of a priest is a source of trouble to the father, and when the difficulty appears to him insurmountable, he applies to this benign god for divine assistance. As soon as their desired objects are accomplished, the worshippers in gratitude visit him, and furnish grand banquets in his name.

A legend tells us that in antiquity, there lived a great potentate named Hiranna Kashupa, whose character was disfigured by odious vices. He had no talent for administration, but had ample share of vicious propensities and sordid avarice. None ventured to whisper in his ear the name of God, for he lived at enmity with the Supreme Being. His retinue and dependents in the palace, were scantily fed and poorly dressed. All his descendants and ascendants were religious men and women. His wife was a model of virtue. His children were taught by a man a true emblem of the character of the monstrous King. His youngest son named Prahlad baffled all the inducements of his father and the teacher. The boy made rapid progress under the tuition of his mother, both in education and in religion. Nature furnished him with a strong and clear understanding, rare firmness of temper and intensity of will. From the beginning of his childhood, he received instructions from his generous mother, in all the several branches of literature and science.

One day having been in company with his brothers, he persuaded them to be religious people and recommended them not to listen to the fallacious instructions, imparted to them by their irreligious teacher. Thereupon all the brothers pronounced Hari (God). Then the fury of the tyrant rose to madness. But all the attempts to destroy Prahlad the youngest and most pious, were fruitless.

CHAPTER VIII.

The attempt of Hiranna Kashapa to kill his youngest son—He himself was killed—A comparison between the Indian and the Rockaway Beach Picnics.

Hiranna Kashapa under the mask of amicability proposed an arrangement; but the boy was a devout servant of God and the man of the Devil, such wide difference admitted of no compromise. The latter ordered his executioner to burn him alive. Accordingly a fire was made and the poor and innocent victim was thrown into it, and Brahma (the god of fire) protected him from harm. The father subsequently ordered the boy should be thrown into the depths of the sea, where the protection of Brahma would be of no avail. Accordingly the executioner fastened him to a huge stone and placed him in a ferry boat. As soon as the boat reached deep water, he dropped him in. But no fear of danger could force him to renounce his fidelity to the Deity Hari. Varuna the god of water made the stone buoyant, and prevented it from sinking. On a stormy day, the enraged and malignant father placed his son on a bracketless tower, tapering high in the air, so that the violence of the wind, might cause him to fall from the perilous height; but Pabana the god of wind stopped the storm. The father took him to a high mountain and dropped him from the top of the most elevated peak, but Vasumati the goddess of earth placed him on her lap. The boy was thrown before a mad elephant, in hopes that he might destroy him, but the Supreme Deity conferred special sensibility upon the mighty animal, which took him up and seated him on his back. The father inquired of his son, "has any one hitherto seen the God?" "Yes," was the reply. The former further questioned, pointing out a room, "Is he in this room?" "Yes" was the reply. The father with excitement asked "Is he in the pillar?" The answer being in the affirmative, the enraged father ordered the pillar to be broken down. The god came out and killed him. He was re-born in three successive times, and on every occasion, he is represented to have been one of the most execrable of human fiends. In his next generation, he appeared on earth as Ravana the demon king of Ceylon. In wealth, rank and education, he had few equals; in cruelty and vice, he was unsurpassed.

Legend tells us that as soon as the father was killed, the boy knelt down with folded hands, and interceded on behalf of his father so that in parakal (next generation), he might prove a better man. The image portraying the sacrilegious deceased and the prayerful boy with folded hands, graphically describes and represents the glorious action, and by this, convinces the Hindus that the god is the encourager of virtue and discourager of vice.

During second generation, Hiranna Kushapa had some reverence for the Creator, whom he addressed as grandfather, and this particular God alone helped him; whereas all men abhorred him and the rest of the gods were inimical to him. He again had a violent death. On account of a virtuous brother named Bivishana, and by the favor of the Creator, he was born a prince for the third and last time.

In the succeeding generation, his name was Kansa a prince who lived at Muttra, on the river Jumna. It was foretold that his nephew would kill him. Accordingly he imprisoned his sister Daboki and her husband Basudeva, in hopes of being able to kill the baby as soon as it was born or to kill the prisoners by starvation. He provided them with such scanty food, as to reduce them almost to skeletons. On the birth of the much expected baby, the father removed him to Brindabana, and a baby girl was substituted. The latter was snatched away from her new mother's arm when she assumed the form of a kite, (hence a kite is regarded as sacred) and fled away. All the male babies, according to the order of the king, were put to the sword in hopes· that his own nephew would be numbered with the slain. But this hope was frustrated by his being promptly removed to the aforesaid place where in the house of a milkman named Nanda, the baby flourished in company with the shepherd boys. He was nominated Krishna who addressed his host and hostess as parents.

He sat on the same bench with the lower class of boys, ate the same food, grazed the same cattle, lived in the same huts and studied the same books or more appropriately the same language; but nothing indicated the greatness to which he was destined, and that none believed that he was the nearest relative of their King.

Rumours, however, reached the suspicious ear of the King, about the survival and the whereabouts of his nephew. Accordingly he sent a woman named Putna to destroy him by poison. Her purpose was discovered and she was put to death. Aghasoora and Boghasoora undertook similar enterprise and shared the same fate. When the boy arrived at maturity, he waged war with his uncle, and slew him with his army. His parents were liberated, and the military and civil administrations were reformed.

Thus the man was born three times and was killed. As he never made a prominent figure again in the Indian history or fiction, I consider, he was allotted, by the supreme Magistrate, a birth either in animal species or in the family of a lower caste.

When a child is born, it is taken to Nrishingha. His father, with a large number of his friends and relatives amounting sometimes to five hundred, go to this great religious sanctuary either in carriages, palankeens or in bullock trains. The household priest always leads the van. He appoints a number of priestly caste men to cook food under his supervision. Their cooked food could be conveniently shared by all, but that cooked by any other sect, would be useful only to that particular sect, as in

India the one caste does not use the food of the other, but that cooked by the priests can be conveniently consumed by all.

When milkmen appear with their milk before the shrine, no matter what their reputed practice (they increase the quantity of milk with the mixture of water) on other occasions, bring pure milk, since deception on such an occasion would provoke the anger of the god. His house is situated in a fine grove consisting of the tamarind, jack, mango and the majestic banyan. There are no benches beneath the trees, but people take with them long sheets to spread upon the ground where they sit.

When the congregation is engaged in play, conversation and other amusements, the priests engage in the preparation of rice, which is cooked, on this special occasion, with milk and sugar (as in Europe and America), in large earthen vessels. When prepared, they are placed before the god and the door is securely fastened, so that none should see him when he takes his meal. When he finishes, all the vessels containing the residue, are brought and distributed to the people on large plantation leaves placed on the floor. When the priests finish, the Kyasthu, followed by various other classes sit. Towards the close of the evening they return homewards.

In contrast to the above fact I may remark, that when I visited some friends of Rockaway Beach U. S. America last year, I was invited to a picnic on an island about six miles distant. At morning I visited a religious lady named Mrs. Brooks, to whom I am indebted for the kind invitation. It had been arranged that all should meet in the school building. So I hastened to the school where after a short mutual conversation, we walked towards the wharf for a ferry. Prior to this, Miss Brook the daughter of the lady above described, at the suggestion of Mr. Frase, who bore a leading part in this affair, furnished me with a blue ribbon temperance badge. In an instant, the ladies and gentlemen, boys and girls assembled in the dock, and awaited the arrival of a ferry. It anon appeared and was loaded with the assembled population. During the short passage across the water, Long Island, with its rows of buildings more or less shaded by the varied tints of foliage, then in all leafy luxuriance of July, formed a pleasing attraction to the eyes; whilst the delightful songs of the gay children and their recitations at intervals, were no less harmonious to the ears of the passengers, during their brief trip.

We landed on the shore of a fine grove which I had never previously visited, and by open car proceeded to a neighbouring village, where benches and tables were amply provided, under the genial shade of Nature's umbrageous plumes. Whilst the majority of the adults rested, the children delighted us with their vivacity, swinging, singing, running foot-races and engaged in the varied childish games, which are always recalled with feelings of pleasure in after life but are fitted during childhood only, a bell announced the hour of repast which was doled out in the following methodical order :—the children were served first, then the ladies and ultimately the adults of the sterner sex.

I found myself the subject of special hospitality, for noticing my partiality for fresh milk Mr. and Mrs. Brooks supplied me plenteously, and on Mr. Frase's inquiring how I had fared, my expression of satisfaction mirrored my appreciation. Not until all others of our picnic party had finished, did the parsons sit to their meal, and on my mentioning to Mr. Frase that " the custom here is entirely different from ours, as our priests always secure precedence in a feast," he smiled and said " we feed our children first."

Mr. Ratan, a member of the choir, sang and his example was followed by Mr. Henderickson and ultimately by all present. On account of my being an indifferent vocalist, my apology for not joining them was accepted. Whilst professional singers are heard with judicial appreciation, amateurs are not, as a rule, greatly valued, but the members of the party sang so beautifully and melodiously, as to attract the attention of all.

The exactitude of respect demanded of young folks in India, prevents their seniors from singing in the presence of their youngsters, which is regarded as too great a familiarity and levity. So tenacious is seniority and its privileges, that a younger brother, be the difference of age ever so little, highly respects his elder and is ready to fulfil his anga or order without question. Joke, laughter and undue familiarity are scarcely displayed by the younger in the presence of his senior brother. The former never smokes in the presence of the latter, and should he, at any time, be so indulging, on the approach of his elder, he conceals his hubble and bubble.* This high respect to the eldest brother alone induced Bhima as previously narrated, to suppress his anger, when the wife of Judishthira, was brought to the court in violation of all the social customs of Hindu society.

The second bell, having announced the time for supper, put an end to the part and solo songs which became gradually not only attractive but highly impressive. The meal was distributed in the same methodical order as before. I was regaled with a large quantity of milk furnished by Mr. and Mrs. Brooks, and with fruits and sugar furnished by other people. Mr. Frase with unfailing equanimity inquired whether I was amply served and my affirmative reply satisfied him. When I finished, I went to a neighbouring apple garden accompanied by some school children, who having known me upwards of two years, wanted to learn something about India. I gave them a description of Indian children, how they are educated, how often in a year they have holidays, what are the principal branches of their studies and other miscellaneous things, to which they listened with great attention.

At the close of the day we started for Rockaway Beach. On our return to the railway station (which is called dépôt in America and the Americans substitute the word "car" for "train.") Mrs. Brooks, being greatly interested in religious rites, ceremonies and practices, inquired about Indian

---

* A hubble bubble is a kind of pipe, the perforated wooden stem of which is about two feet long, and is inserted through a hole in a cocoa nut into an earthenware receptacle, about six inches deep where the tobacco is placed. The water in the nut secures a cool temperature for the smoker.

customs, the way in which the idols are worshipped, how the goats are killed and the guests fed; noticing her great interest, I endeavoured to render my answers as impressive as possible. On returning to Mrs. Henry, a respectable lady of Rockaway Beach, she very kindly assigned to me a large room, free of charge, at a time when the locality (it being a great summer resort) was crowded to the overflowing, and when the rent of even a small room amounted to three dollars (twelve shillings) per night, assuring me that I could use it for weeks.

Although the meals of the picnic party might be considered as a repast of special occasion, I noticed that my American friends took their customary number of meals most regularly, and I am of opinion that the Indian practice of confinement to one meal, in a festivity at three o'clock, is insufficient in the majority of cases to ensure health and strength.

In the grove where our picnic took place there is a commodious building, open on all sides, which although destitute of architectural beauty, admirably served our purpose, as we could repair there in case of a shower of rain. Otherwise we could achieve all our work in open air. But it is to be regretted no similar shelter has been erected contiguous to the house of god Nrishingha, as the worshippers there are sometimes too numerous to have any quarter, during a terrible shower of rain, which bears little resemblance to the vernal showers of Western Europe nay those of U. S. America. So most of the visitors to the shrine being exposed to such rain, pay the penalty of this want of provision by contracting malaria fever and submitting to an untimely death. I say for the good of Hindu community, that there should be erected a convenient building, that can save a person from exposure and its accompanying result.

CHAPTER IX.

Goddess Lakshmi—Goddess Shashthi and goddess Vasuki.

In India gods and goddesses are worshipped. Every Hindu has a household goddess named Lakshmi. She is worshipped four times a year, with offerings of rice and flowers. The priest visits her in every house, chants an anthem called Muntra, salutes her and then withdraws. For this he accepts an offertory of rice, plantain, sweet-meats and cakes to which is added a monetary gift. On his departure the door is secured to enable the goddess to take her meal, without the supervision of human beings.

The origin of her worship could be attributed to the fact that in antiquity, there was a very poor boy of priestly caste, who was in such circumstances of destitution, as to be unable to procure shoes or decent covering. He went from house to house, worshipping gods and goddesses and imploring an amelioration of his condition, but without avail. One day on his way home, he saw a white owl, supposed to be the carrier of the goddess of wealth, seated on the top of a tree. The boy was greatly pleased to see the auspicious bird, and addressed it thus " Pachn nacha Khabi amar duksha ghuchabi" (Oh, owl! will you share my food and remove my distress). The bird conformed to his wishes and took some rice, to please the eagerness of the lad, and flew away, enjoining that on the appearance of the goddess who would be conveyed the next morning, to receive her with befitting solemnity and welcome.

On his return home, the lad informed his mother of what had passed and desired her to do all she could to propitiate the goddess. The boy went away, the next morning, to solicit at the shrines of neighbouring gods, some means of subsistence ; whilst the mother procured a loan of money to buy things, requisite for the reception of the goddess. On its return home, the bird, believing the house of the boy, no favourite resort of its mistress, said nothing of the interview. She for a ride mounted the back of the bird, the following day, and was conveyed, according to its promise, to the house of the boy, but finding it an unsacred place, with every mark of displeasure she was re-conveyed home.

On his return, the boy inquired of his mother whether the goddess visited her, and on receiving a negative reply, he met the bird at the foot of the aforesaid tree and reminded it about the non-fulfilment of its promise. Whereupon the bird replied that, " your mother kept the house so dirty as to provoke the goddess, who renounced all connection with such a dirty woman ; but, however, to-mcrrow I would carry her again, subject to the proviso that you would stay home, and ensure the cleanliness of the house to enable yourself to receive her." Having promised compliance, he returned home. The next morning as soon as the goddess arrived at the house, she was respectfully received and worshipped. Subsequently, by the favour of the goddess the poverty of the boy was removed, and hence throughout India, persons desirous of wealth, pay her special attention.

This worship has one singular effect, that the belief keeps people neat and clean, but cleanliness alone is not sufficient to keep malaria at a distance. Regular meals, whether two or three a day, are essential to invigorate an individual.

The goddess Shushthi sits beneath a tree encircled by almost an impervious jungle. The ladies are very interested in her, as she is the protector of children. The cat is her beloved animal. If any lady kills a cat her children are never blessed with longevity. But the punishment of killing a cow, is by far greater than that prescribed for any other offence. A man who kills another unintentionally, is sentenced to a few months' imprisonment only ; but he who kills a cow unintentionally, is not allowed to speak to anybody for three years. He is forced to reside in a cottage for the above period in a desolate place. The third penalty is that he is constrained to live on beggary, and is restricted to one meal a day. He lives in his enviable boarding house at night, and spends day time in begging from door to door. He need not apply for alms, as the people voluntarily furnish him when they recognize him by his distinguishing badges, a strong rope round his neck and some grass in his mouth. When he visits a house he makes the sound resembling that of a cow. If there be a number of mendicants waiting for alms, the cow-killer has precedence. When the prescribed time expires, he shaves his head, gives a grand banquet and is reinstated. I have experienced only one case, in which a lady accidentally killed a calf. I saw her with the badges in the outer premises of a house, she took the grass described above, out of her mouth and made the sound, the owner thereupon in a great hurry satisfied her requirement and she withdrew. I have already mentioned a lady is not allowed to go out, but in this case she is not entitled to stay in. She was reinstated at the end of the fixed time, after a ceremony. A gentleman on my inquiry, informed me that whosoever accidentally kills a cow and conceals the offence, finds that his meals are besmeared with cow-blood, so he must submit to the penalty.

The ladies repair (this freedom is granted them during the festivity) to the jungle with their household priests and worship her in due order, first the priestly caste and secondly the Kyasthu, and finally the lower class.

In another jungle a goddess named Shitala, the goddess of small pox resides. It is believed whosoever neglects to worship her, dies of small pox. Once a man broke her residence and the death of his son was attributed to the anger of this goddess.

Vasuki the goddess, of snakes, is also worshipped. Singularly enough in this particular worship the priests have no participations ; and the offerings which are customarily sent to the priests, are generally sent to the house of a carpenter, a Sudra, or servile caste.

On account of the deadly bites, the divine power is attributed to this goddess, hence she is regarded as a fitting object of reverence. I know nothing personally about the divine power of a serpent, but I can say, that India abounds with a countless variety and that the annual mortality, from snake bites is immense. The worship is said to have originated thus :—

In antiquity, there lived a Banyan named Chando Sudagor (merchant). He never believed in the divine right of Vasuki. He had six sons whom he long detained at home, for fear that Chang Muri (a contemptuous name given her by the man) should do them some injury. At length circumstances forced him to send them to a distant country to fetch goods. The difficulties of land route induced them to go by sea. The goddess raised a fearful storm in which they were all lost, together with their goods. This catastrophe affected Chando beyond all description.

After a long time, he had another son named Lakshmindara, whose personal beauty so well accorded, with the excellence of his character as to procure for him, the name " Sonar (golden) Lakshmindara." It was fore-told in the Shastras (holy Indian book), that on the night of his marriage he would die of a serpent-bite. Chando, more willing to keep his only son single, than to propitiate the serpent-goddess, raised obstacle to his son's marriage. When he arrived at an advanced age, public censure forced the father to give way and a girl named Baolo was selected. On an auspicious day* Chando according to the customary rule, accompanied by a large number of his people repaired to the house of the father of the bride. It always happens that both parties should assemble in a large hall where a literary debate between the children of two parties is always encouraged. Anon the father of the bride comes and removes the bridegroom to the con-gregation of the ladies assembled in the inner premises of

---

* The day is ascertained out of a religious book by the priests. In some months, as for instance, December there is no marriage so the betrothed couple must wait till January. Marriage cannot be legalized in all the days in a week but on a prescribed day, which none but the sages and the pundits can ascertain.

F

the house, with the sanction of the men. After the marriage is over, the couple repair to a room, accompanied by the ladies of the neighbourhood. This ceremony was repeated excepting that, the father of the bride being apprised of the prophecy, built an iron room where the pair alone repaired, and the door was fastened. The exclusion of the ladies, in this instance could be attributed to the fact, that their admission would necessitate the repeated opening of the door, when perchance some serpent might enter unobserved and effect a bite.

The bridegroom slumbered, but the sleepless bride, revolving in her troubled mind, the fate to which her husband was destined, sought to discover some mode to elude the prophecy. Restless as she was, she peeped out and saw an immense number of serpents hanging round the room. Upon which, she opened the massive iron door and feigning fearlessness, sought an acquaintance with one of them and inquired in her kindest voice, " How was it possible, that you being so huge proportioned animals " for some of the snakes of India are 30 feet in length " could live in a small place? " The serpent declared that in case of necessity, they could shorten their bodies, when she expressed the greatest surprise and entreated them to show her how could they fulfil this object. She immediately produced a large silver vase of antique pattern, and at her request they all confidently entered and were securely fastened. Having frustrated the plan of the enemy, she retired to rest and was involved in profound sleep.

On hearing the defeat of the prophecy and the capture of her subjects, the goddess wept most bitterly, bemoaning that no more snakes remained to fulfil the prediction. At length remembering that she still had an old and faithful reptile, on which she could rely, she commissioned it for the fulfilment of the object. The serpent made every attempt to break through but instead of succeeding in this attempt, it broke its teeth which bled fearfully. It returned, and representing its inability to effect an entrance, greatly mortified the baffled goddess, who now besought the aid of gods. Her prayer and supplication were heard and a piece of white thread was dropped on the large serpent.

The thread became a thin white snake.* At the request of the goddess it repaired to the place. Now here commences a dismal tragedy. The room was not built by an American workman, but by a superstitious Indian ironsmith, who dreading the anger of the goddess, left a very small hole, unknown to the owner, which could admit only a thin needle. By this it entered and inflicted a deadly bite on the golden Lakshmindara, from the effect of which he was soon killed.

Nothing could exceed the sorrow of the girl to whom widow-marriage was quite unknown, than to see the lifeless body of that one, to protect whom she had left no stone unturned. She piteously bemoaned the loss, and accused the goddess of sleep, whose intervention was the cause of her husband's death, as she justly remarked that in the absence of sleep, she would have succeeded in devising some means to baffle the prediction. Whereas the husband died, she thought some mode whereby he could be restored.

She conveyed the body to the Ganges, took her father's boat and set sail, with a view to proceed thither where the merciful Almighty directs her. The next day she found a human habitation, left the corpse behind and became the guest of the mistress who, on being informed of the doleful history of the tragic death, expressed her kindest sympathy.

During the interview the mistress was much disturbed by her little boy, and giving way to an impulse she suddenly seized the only child and thrust him into the blazing fire, to the terrified horror of the young widow. In reply to the exclamations of agony of the visitor, the mistress made reply that she simply sent the child to sleep. Then taking a few drops of water and sprinkling the fire, she reproduced her boy. Astonished at the manifestation of such stupendous and surprising power, the widow entreated her kindly to awake her sleeping husband. At her request Baolo brought the corpse, but unfortunately the former

---

* During my boyhood, I brought up a bird which one day flew to a neighbouring jungle. I fetched it and found a piece of white thread in its bill. A lady advised me to crush it, saying it was a small snake. I crushed it, but the bird subsequently died.

failed to accomplish this object, as the body had been mutilated, and a part of it was destroyed by some animal, whilst placed in the boat unprotected.

The mistress taught her guest dancing, and sent her to the palace of Debraj Indra, the King of gods, where she so far succeeded in delighting the divine King by her grace and proficiency, that he desired her to name some gift he should proffer. Upon this she implored that her husband should be restored to her, which request was readily granted. The girl heartily thanked Debray and returned to her hostess and expressed her gratitude for her kindly advice. The husband who knew nothing of his tragic death and restoration, was quite astonished to see that he was transferred into a different place during his sleep, as he thought that he was in the company of two strangers. The husband, according to the Indian custom, never sees his wife before the marriage is complete and before the wife is removed to the husband's house.*

The faithful wife informed him all that had passed, during his long sleep and how he had been restored, upon which the husband expressed his gratitude in recognition of her ever-memorable service, and being accompanied by his wife, repaired to the residence of his father. Through the intercession of the gifted girl, a reconciliation took place between the enraged Vasuki and the wronged father. The latter propitiated the goddess, by worshipping, who restored his six sons together with their goods. Hence the Hindus worship the snakes.

---

* When the bride entered the iron room she had a veil over her face which rendered it impossible for the husband to see the wife. But when the husband saw them in the house they were without veils, as he was dead, and no lady uses her veil in the presence of a corpse. Our customs are so alien to those of others, that we encounter considerable difficulties in making our facts explicit to those, who have no share of personal knowledge of our customs.

CHAPTER X.

The description of Rama, incarnation of Vishnu, and the origin of the worship of goddess Durga.

The idea of worshipping all the gods and goddesses has been inherited from our Aryan* forefathers, who founded Benares, which was a most important and flourishing place anterior to the dawn of the regular history of the world. It is the Mecca of the Hindus, but the obscurity of its antiquity, makes it difficult for us to distinguish facts from fictions. The valiant feats of strength attributed to Bhima, such as his carrying five persons on his shoulders at one time, and other heroic actions must not be dismissed as incredible, whilst I have seen in the museum of Rockaway Beach, is exhibited a gigantic Patagonian, measuring from top to toe 14 feet. On the pedestal of this exhibit is a statement, that another museum contains the skeleton of a giant eleven feet in height. Bhima, if of similar size, and endowed with corresponding strength, might have been equal to such a task, is a fact which could be proved by the clearest evidences. No doubt the discovery of the fossils of the antediluvian period, has much to do with the legends and belief in the colossal proportions of men during the earlier ages. Still the discovery of weapons of a kind such as could only be used by men of gigantic size and immense strength, must evidence the existence of exceptional individuals. Some years elapsed, a British

* The Aryan or Indo-European peoples are those by whom, the Sanskrit, Greek, Latin, Gothic and Celtic languages are employed.

officer discovered, at the foot of the Himalaya, a bow far too large and too heavy to permit of its use by the strongest men of the present day.   In November, on board the S.S. " City of New York," *en route* to Liverpool, I had the pleasure of entering into a disputative argument with Colonel Sadler, a gentleman of highest military distinction in England, about the bridge that connected one day Ceylon and India.   It was a long bridge suspended by Rama in antiquity to effect a passage of his troops across the sea, and to this day it has been a great obstacle to the movement of a vessel which, owing to the remains of the bridge, sails for Europe by doubling Ceylon.   However, to my intelligent readers I leave the task of distinguishing facts from fictions.

The   origin   of   the   sacred   attributes   of   the   monkey is as follows :—Rama, the incarnation of Vishnu,* was born in the palace of Dasharatha, a great potentate of antiquity, who had three wives.   When Kaikai the most beloved of them, heard that Rama, the eldest and most devout, would, according   to   the   rules   of   primogeniture,   succeed,   she exercised her influence on the enslaved King in favour of her only son Bharata, and fearing the popularity of Rama might induce his adherents to draw sword on his behalf if he allowed to reside in the palace, she pursuaded the monarch to banish him for fourteen years.   On hearing the rigorous sentence, which had been passed upon him, he exchanged his royal robe for that of a religious devotee, and accompanied by his wife and step-brother, Lakshmana, left the kingdom.   He crossed the Ganges and lived in a ungle where his subsistence was dependent upon his manual labour.

---

* Vishnu the preserver, Brahma the Creator and Siva the de-stroyer.   The three form trinity ; as God the Father, God the Son and God the Holy Ghost.   They are supreme ; all are worshipped save the Creator for the following reason :—he has a quarrelsome son named Narada whose profession is "quarrel."   No one pro-nounces his name for the fear of a mishappening.   He visits a house or a congregation with intent to effect a breach.   The mischievous conduct of the son provoked the father who chastised him.   The son, in revenge, issued a proclamation preventing people from worshipping the father.

On the death of Dasharatha, Bharata, the then reigning King, proceeded to the jungle and representing Rama the exiled prince, about the death of his father and the disturbed condition of the country, in vain endeavoured to induce him to return and accept the sovereignty. Disappointed in this mission, he placed the wooden shoes of his elder stepbrother (Rama), on the throne and managed the kingdom for the *interim*, as guardian of the shoes. Rama built two cottages, the one for himself and the other for his brother. In this jungle named Punchabati, they comfortably resided, until their happiness was disturbed by Surpanakha the cannibal princess of Ceylon, who desired that the one or the other should marry her; but was greatly provoked at the refusal of her overtures. Enraged at the conduct of Rama, she made an attempt upon the life of his wife, for the punishment of her husband's denial. Lakshmana mutilated her by cutting off her nose and ears. The disfigured, mutilated and bleeding princess appealed to her brothers Khara and Dushana, who were governing that part of India as Viceroys of Ravana. They led the van of a large army for chastising the transgressor, but were successfully repelled in a sharp encounter, in spite of their numerical superiority and at length were vanquished and dispersed. The princess having failed in this, placed her case before her brother Ravana the demoniac, whose name has already been mentioned, of Ceylon. Aware in his inability, to cope with his mighty enemy in the field, he resorted to a stratagem and begged Marich, one of his courtiers to assist him by assuming the appearance of a golden deer.

To satisfy the King, Marich appeared on the premises of the cottage, in the shape of a golden deer. The simplehearted Sitta, fascinated by the graceful play of the beautiful animal, in front of her cottage, easily succeeded in persuading her husband to capture it. Upon following the animal into a thick jungle for that purpose, Rama was astounded to see it suddenly resumed the form of a man and loudly cried for help from Lakshmana, representing that the deer had jeopardized his (Rama's) life. Lakshmana discredited the fact and hesitated to leave Sitta, when she fearing the danger of her husband, permitted him to go and remove her husband's difficulty. Accordingly he repaired to the jungle and saw Rama killed the disguised man.

In the meantime, Ravana well aware that by the success of his decoy, the girl has been left unprotected, he assumed the garb of a religious mendicant, visited the cottage and implored for alms. Influenced by the religious obligation of extending hospitality to all, especially to a jogi (sage) mendicant and unsuspicious of harm, she approached the disguised beggar, upon which she was seized and conveyed across the sea to Ceylon.

The melancholy news was soon noised about and great sympathy was felt for the abducted wife. A neighbouring prince named Sugriva, who had been dethroned by a faction of his subjects, headed by his brother Baly, promised in the event of Rama assisting him to regain his throne, to place his entire army at his disposal, for the recovery of Sitta and the punishment of Ravana.

Rama accepted the proposal, and with only a handful of army dethroned and slew the usurper and restored Sugriva. By this success Rama won the confidence of all the neighbouring princes, who placed their troops at his disposal. Hanuman, a monkey-general of the army of Sugriva, was selected and advised to proceed for reconnoitring. Having carefully ascertained Ceylon was the place of the detention of Sitta, he took the ring of Rama as an indication that he had come from him, and repaired thither. He visited, delivered the ring which Sitta could easily recognise as belonging to Rama, and was regaled with delicious mango, but his appetite being unappeased, he reached a mango-grove in search of more. The curious animal, as he appeared to the cannibals, gained their favourable opinion by his feats of agility. Believing he would protect their fruits from the predatory birds, they entrusted to him the care of their garden and went to dinner. Taking advantage of their absence, he ate some mangoes, destroyed the rest and at length uprooted the trees. On their return, a scuffle ensued in which many of them, including Aukhoy, one of the sons of Ravana, were slain. Indrajata, the second son, overpowered and captured the animal and carried him home in triumph. Intending to burn him alive, linen cloths, drenched with oil, were wrapped round him and were subsequently set on fire. The monkey enveloped in the flames, jumped upon the thatched roof of a house, which immediately ignited and then jumping from the one to the other, he soon kindled a great conflagration. Having effected all the mischief possible, he jumped into the sea and regained the mainland.

The intercession of Bivishana, the pious brother of the King, although earnestly seconded by those of his wife, failed to induce him to surrender Sitta to her lord. At length the queen pursuaded Ravana to play a game of chess with her, on condition that, should she be successful, he would accede to her wishes and liberate his captive. This is said to be the origin of chess. The queen won it and urged him to desist; but his fury being unrestrained he assaulted his brother (for his giving such advice), who joined the enemy.

The success of Hanumana greatly satisfied Rama, who became the captain-general of the allied army and appointed the monkey his assistant and superintendent of the construction of the bridge, which was built up to facilitate the movement of the army. They reached the opposite shore unopposed. At length the war was declared and the troops of the enemy became unsuccessful in every engagement excepting those encounters of which Ravana himself assumed the chief command. In a battle Ravana prostrated both Rama and his brother, who became senseless. On their recovery, they rallied their troops and returning to the charge, created a dreadful havoc, killing almost all the best generals of the enemy. Kumvakarna (a great giant) and Taruni Sen (the pious son of Bivishana) were numbered among the slain. Upon which the troops of Indrajita ran to the thickest of the charge, slew and dispersed them all. He himself fought with great valour, prostrated the two brothers and made a triumphant entry into his father's palace. The next day the brothers having recovered, conducted the battle with unflagging zeal. The enemy retreated with considerable loss. Indrajita rallied them and renewed the engagement. This man was such a great warrior as to frighten even Debraj Indra himself the King of gods. The troops of Rama could not stand the well-directed arrows of the enemy. Most of them were killed and some ran away. The remainder including the two brothers left senseless on the ground In the first and second battle, of which the chief command was entrusted to Indrajita, he fared well and during the third engagement, he was accidentally killed by an arrow from Lakshmana.

Mahiravana, another son of Ravana, succeeded his deceased brother. By a stratagem, he defeated the troops of the enemy, captured the two brothers and conveyed them to Patal (modern America) intending to sacrifice them before his household goddess, and thereby to put an end to the war. The monkey searched for them in every part of the globe and at length visited Patal. Greatly perplexed as to how and where to proceed in quest of the lost ones, he climbed and sat on the top of a tree. He overheard two young ladies who were passing and conversing, about the youths and the shrine which was the place of their confinement. The monkey accordingly proceeded to the royal shrine, and found them bound at the foot of the goddess. He demanded her sword but on refusal, he placed her on his head and threatened to plunge her into the Atlantic. Under these threats, the goddess complied, and promised no longer to support the cannibal prince. On the approach of the latter, the monkey concealed himself. Mahiravana unsuspectingly prostrated in adoration of the goddess, when the monkey took her sword and severed the head of the man from his body. He unfastened the brothers and accompanied them to the rendezvous of Ceylon. Ravana again appeared at the head of his army and in one of his successful engagements Rama and his brother were wounded, and again fell senseless on the field. Susena the doctor, dressed the wounds and prescribed some medicinal herbs which could only be found in the Himalaya. He further added in the absence of such medicine, they would perish before the sun-rise. With mysterious satisfaction, Ravana learned from his spy what the doctor said and commanded the sun to rise without delay.

The monkey was sent to the Himalaya in search of medicine. He reached the place of his destination, where he met a sage to whom he represented what had passed. The sage furnished him food, and requested to purify himself by an immersion in a neighbouring tank. The monkey plunged into the water and was attacked by a crocodile, which was immediately killed. The reptile assumed the form of a god, warned him of the false sage whom Ravana had placed there for some mischievous purpose and disappeared. The monkey forewarned of his treacherous host, rushed upon him and slew him. Having failed to discover the herbs, he took the mountain upon his head and started. On his way, he found the sun was attempting to rise before his usual hour, so he caught him and put him in his pocket. Having secured the death of Rama* in his pocket, he thought himself quite free to test the strength of Bharata the above described reigning half brother of Rama, so he went to his capital Ajodha. Seeing the approach of some stupendous thing Bharata fired and the monkey fell senseless on the ground. On recovery he related the fall of Rama and started for Ceylon.

The application of the medicine restored the brothers and the sun was allowed to rise. The combat was renewed and Ravana who had ten heads and twenty hands lost nine heads which instantaneously resumed their places. Some hands were chopped and were similarly restored. This greatly astonished Rama who subsequently discovered the means which could complete the destruction of the monster. The monkey was sent to bring Ravana's death arrow† which was concealed in the house of Ravana. In the garb of a sage, the monkey reached the palace with

---

* The wound of Rama was mortal at sunrise but the sun would not rise at all unless he was set free. It was on this consideration the monkey thought he was quite free to proceed wherever he liked.

† This arrow had a long history the description of which, for the want of space, I beg to reserve for some future opportune moment.

a nicely bound Shastrus to prophecy some favorable issue of the war. Mondadari, the wife of Ravana, cordially received him and conversed with him. He read a passage out of the book, and interpreted to mean that the danger would soon be over, and that she should not display any anxiety, whilst the death-arrow remained carefully concealed in her house. Only a few most reliable people knew the existence of it, but none knew where it was concealed. The pretended prophet further requested her not to allow anybody to handle it for fear some emissary of the enemy might take it away, upon which she said, " handling was impossible as it had been built up in the hollow pillar " pointing it out at the same time. Hardly had she finished this, the false prophet became metamorphosed into a huge monkey, who with a vigorous kick broke the pillar, took the arrow and departed

Rama received it with great joy, but still his difficulty was not over, as Ravana was protected by Durga (the wife of Siva), the household goddess of Ravana. Rama had to propitiate her by worship; accordingly he sent the monkey to the Himalaya to bring 108 red lilies which were not procurable elsewhere. An image was made and the goddess appeared in it. With a view to try the earnest devotion of Rama, she stole one of the flowers, upon which Rama resolved to knock her eyes out and place them at her feet, in substitution of the lost one. Without putting him to the test of such a sacrifice, the goddess was propitiated, and permission was given to destroy the enemy. The battle was renewed and Ravana fell and Bivishana was placed on the throne. Rama subsequently finished the period of his transportation, and on his return home with his wife and brother succeeded to the vacant throne. Owing to the kindly help, the image of the goddess is worshipped in India and the people believe that she appears in the image and answers their prayers. She is celebrated during October with great pomp. The monkey having benefitted mankind, he and his descendants have been recognised as sacred, but cows are considered much more so, as she is supposed to be the wife of the same god, and both Durga and a cow are adored with equal respect and devotion.

CHAPTER XI.

My career in the United States of America.

The limited time and space precluded the possibility of fully describing the curious legendary origins of many of the Indian deities. However, on some future day if it be the will of the Almighty Father, I intend to write a concise Indian history, descriptive of ancient and modern facts. My efforts in this direction will be restricted by the margin of my means, and although before my departure for England my countrymen, who were most liberal in their proffered assistance, have proved no more reliable than those " who keep the word of promise to our ear and break it to our hope," I am far from being discouraged of the future. I have encountered considerable difficulties at times but strict economy has enabled me to defray the expenses, not only of my studies, but those of my rice and salt. It is the mistaken belief of my countrymen that an Indian cannot live in England without meat and liquor. To undeceive them, I beg to say that in my travels I have visited cities, towns and villages where the snow-fall amounted to thirteen feet deep at places, but still I could thrive on Indian rice and dal, and thanked God who furnished them in such abundance, that I have never experienced want although my position is not at all enviable, as I have to fill four different offices at the same time. The office of earning money is assigned in India to the *paterfamilias*, and I have to earn money for my own subsistence ; to buy things in a market is an office performed by servants and I myself am to do it ; the ladies cook food for their household people and I am to do so for myself ; the work of studies is confined to the student of the household and I am to study for completing my own education. Consequently I can devote only my leisure hour to my studies. This is not the worst, because the weakness of my eyes, the left one of which has twice been operated by Moorfield's Hospital, forces me to the constant resort to hospital wherever I roam.

My work in the U. S. America is of material assistance to me. During last summer I visited Syracuse and pro- cured a temporary position in the main office Western Union Company. Whilst I resided there I had the pleasure of visiting some eminent persons, such as Hon, Hiscock, American senator and eminent lawyer, Dr. Vernon who very graciously promised me an introduction to the president of the University College at the beginning of the winter session, and other gentlemen. Once I was invited in the Mead's College to address a meeting on temperance. I was greatly pleased to learn the audience was desirous that I should again ascend their platform, but Mr. Behardt the manager of the office, having secured for me a pass to New York, I left Syracuse, assuring them that on some future day I shall again have the pleasure of addressing them.

On my arrival in New York, Mr. Cochrane, the superin- tendent of the Postal Telegraph, being away, I saw Miss Farmer, who said the gentleman is away on his holidays, but on his arrival, " I guess he would employ you." This lady always guesses something good, as I remember when I applied to Mr. Cochrane for an introductory note to Mr. Patangile, Superintendent of Boston, Mass., she said, with her usual kind deportment, " I guess he would give you." Mr. Cochrane obliged me with the intended note. I have a great friend named Mr. J. Glover, now a lawyer in Edinburgh. Whosoever applies him for a position, hears that it is the harvest time of employment and by this kindly expression he does much good to the applicant as he searches with great zeal and ultimately succeeds. The sympathy which this lady displays, ensures the applicant the approach of harvest time, whereupon, after a strenuous exertion he finds suitable employment.

At the recommendation of Mr. Cochrane, on his arrival I was re-appointed by Mr. McClary at 91 Wall Street. Whilst I worked there I visited the main office, and Mr. Shirly, assistant manager, appointed me as night operator ; thus I had the pleasure of working in two offices at the same time. Mr. Shirley, who together with several of the chiefs took most kindly interest in my welfare, received from Mr. McKierman, chief, the following letter on my behalf :—

MR. SHIRLEY ;

Mr. Sarbadhicary has worked under me and has managed his work very well, although he is a stranger to our office. He is fully entitled to the pay of the day in dispute.

Yours truly,

Main Office,   ——McKIERMAN.
11th October, 1889.

I am very much obliged to Mr. McClary for the following kindly certificate :—

91 WALL STREET.

Mr. Sarbadhicary was employed in this office as an operator. He is a scholar and a man of unusual intellect. He is also the author of several books. He is about to proceed to England to complete his legal education.

JAS. A. McCLARY.
18th October, 1889.   *Manager*

A word as to the telegraph reformation achieved by this gentleman, should not be passed over in silence, as his amalgamation of telegraph and caligraph has effected an undeniable success, for, by this arrangement, the customers are furnished with printed messages, an advantage which will never fail to be appreciated by the public.

My best thanks are due to Miss Farmer, Mr. McClary, Mr. Shirley, Mr. Casey, Mr. Talavtal, editor, New York, Messrs. Riker and Pardee of Syracuse, Mr. Sabold, Manager of Albany, Mr. Smith, (chief train despatcher), Boston, Mass., Mr. Gordon, (Superintendent General Postal Telegraph Office) and Miss Nichols of London, Mr. Gray, Chief Superintendent Postal Telegraph Office, Edinburgh, and Mr. Barker, (Assistant Superintendent), Madeira Africa, for their kindly offices, in disposing, on my behalf, of the books which I have the pleasure of writing, in the last year. Having proposed that I should write a book on India, the undermentioned gentlemen, have very kindly subscribed to encourage me and the publication.

1. Mr. Jas. A. McClary, Manager,	2 dollars or 8s.	{ splendid English money { object
2. ,, L.M.	2	,
3. ,, A. King	2	,,
4. ,, Earl	2	,,
5. ,, R. G. W.	2	,
6. ,, Williams	2	
7. ,, Hubbard Precious	2	,,
8. ,, N. Bank Manager	2	,
9. ,, J. B. Taltaval, Editor	2	,,
10. ,, W. P. Philips.Superintendent	2	,,
11. ,, A. B. Chandler, President	2	,,
12. Dr. W. S. Stratford,Professor	2	,,
13. Dr. H. T. Peck, Professor	2	,,

Total 26 Dollars or £6 10s,

Before I set sail for England, I had the pleasure of visiting Hon. G. Cleveland, late President, who very kindly inquired about the Hindu law, and the method of carrying out sentences in the Courts of India. After some further conversation, I advanced the Irish question, " Home Rule for Ireland," saying that Mr. Gladstone is quite willing to give, as large share of local autonomy as the expression implies with a view to unite her more closely, not by legal bonds but by the indissoluble ties of kindly interest and friendship, so that the immemorial race-distinction is superseded by a feeling of sympathy and affection. Thereupon he said " Mr. Gladstone is sure to give it to the Irish." He appears to be much interested in the welfare of the Irish people.

My frequent recurrence to American incidents may lead some of my readers to think that, I have undertaken to write an account of India and not that of America, any mention of the latter is intrusive. In respond to this, I beg to say, that on some future day, I hope to return to India where it is quite possible that I might converse about my books with some Hindu people, who would decidedly discredit my statement as there is a highly educated gentleman named Dr. S. Sarbadhicary. I am of course, quite indifferent as to individual opinions, nor should I regret to see an article in one of the vernacular newspapers confusing the personality of two individuals of the same name, but what I regret the most is that the people will pass contemptuous remarks saying, that a man has returned from England, who falsely claims the authorship of a book written by the doctor. In India, a man without money has no status. If he be a very good speaker, he is regarded as phasil (talkative). If he be a mild man he is considered timid. If he be a thoroughly educated man, his education in the popular estimation is of no avail. When he rises to address a public meeting, although he might be a man of recognised merit, he obtains no hearing.

I am very sorry to have such opinion of my country, but as this opinion has been formed after a good deal of observation, it should not be considered as premature.

Once I had the pleasure of delivering an address, in support of the Punjab University College, Lahore. The next morning it appeared in a journal named *Civil and Military Gazette*, but as it did not specify which of the two persons of the same name (Babu Sasi Bhashan) delivered, it was rumoured that Professor Sasi Bhashan delivered a fine speech, nor could I successfully contradict it, as the number against me was quite numerous, although I knew the gentleman in question was not only not present in the meeting, but that he was absent from Lahore on that evening, at a festival in a neighbouring village named. Meanmeer. Thus the noble professor enjoyed the music and dancing and good cheer provided, in addition to the popular praise for a platform address, and I, who had no share in the pleasures of the festivity, had to join his admirers to praise him for the speech which he had not delivered, lest my silence might be construed into a jealousy of his abilities.

It might be further asked that identification of the doctor and myself should, however, present no difficulties, as Dr. Sarbadhicary is a medical man, consequently he is no telegraphist, he hardly visited any place beyond Bengal, so how should such confusion occur? In reply to this I

G

beg to say that people do not observe facts so minutely ; had they done so, they could easily distinguish the one from the other. Professor Sasi Bhushan rarely attends a public meeting, and should he do so, he very seldom remarks on the subject of discussion. He is a great mathematician and is thoroughly conversant with the science which treats of magnitude and number, and readily solves a problem, to accomplish which some other professors might take hours. Further, the Professor is a member of the Calcutta University, and would not attend to or add a word on behalf of a meeting convened by men of the (adverse) Punjab University. Fearing my countrymen might overlook these distinctions, I have initialed my writing by reference to my second American trip.

CHAPTER XII.

My departure—The description of Karna and the description of
Sributhsha—Conclusion.

I left New York by S.S. City of New York; but after
steaming a short distance a thick fog forced her to anchor.
In the inconvenience of the detention we were not the only
sufferers, for many vessels already anchored and others
inclusive of the renowned Teutonic, one of the fastest
mail steamers in existence, followed the example. The
bold departure of the latter, created great impatience
among the passengers who bitterly exclaimed the over-
cautiousness of our captain. Some said he was not an
enterprising man; some remarked he wanted moral
courage, some said he would have been wise, had he
booked his passage by Teutonic, and whilst the air was
filled by the low mutterings of fierce resentment, a discharge of five successive guns announced the apprehended
danger of Teutonic and secured the popular good opinion
on hehalf of our captain. The very men who accused him
of his culpable dilatoriness, said our captain is a very
sagacious man and his prudence justifies the confidence of
the company which has entrusted to him the magnificent
vessel. His wisdom favorably contrasts that of the
inconsiderate commander of Teutonic, who now finds it
necessary to curb his venturesome daring and submits to
the exigencies of the weather.

This instability of public opinion is a feature of social
history. Macaulay tells us of a person who had partaken
of a poisonous fruit, the reputed effect of which when made

known to him, caused him to regret his rash and thought-less action ; but he anon perceived that it had cured him of a chronic complaint, from which he had suffered for years, whereupon he claimed a popular acknowledgment of the sagacity of his action and the merits of his discovery. The rise and the fall of popular belief is as constant as the tide and the ebb of the sea.

Our troubles did not terminate with the subsidence of the fog ; for after proceeding a short distance an important pin of the machinery broke, and as the rectification was impossible at sea, the vessel was restricted to the use of one engine only.

To enliven the monotony on board the ship, we had several meetings, in one of which, I had the pleasure of delivering a short address on India. By special request, on 20th of November last, I had the pleasure of addressing another meeting on the same subject in the second class saloon. On the following afternoon at the desire of Colonel Sadler, an officer in the Army of Her Majesty's Service, now resident at Preston-on-Tees, Darlington, I had great pleasure of addressing in the first class saloon an appreciative audience consisting of Mr. Justice Proudfoot, Chief Justice of Queen's Bench, Toronto Canada, Mr. R. W. Lewis the United States Consul at Morocco, Colonel and Mrs. Sadler, Miss Hylton a lady who graces a select circle, to which none but the highly privileged have admission in London, Rev. A. S. Lyone, a deservedly popular Irish Minister, and many other ladies and gentlemen. I spoke on India past and present, its myths, traditions, history in commercial and social aspects, carefully avoiding such incidents as have been discussed in previous meetings. At the conclusion Miss Hylton kindly presented me with a £5 note saying, this is in recognition of your most interesting lecture. The pleasure of this *douceur* was greatly enhanced, by the interest with which I had been listened to. The above mentioned Colonel, and a lawyer of New York whose name greatly to my regret I have forgotten, deserve my heartiest thanks for the warm interest with which they introduced me to the meeting. It was known to the audience that I was about to write a book on India ; accordingly, they give me many a gracious promise of encouragement.

The idea of my speaking on board the ship arose thus :—
On my way to New York by S.S. City of Paris, I saw some passengers of the second-class found fault with everything the crew provided. Accordingly they were about to send a petition to the Captain complaining that they were not amply fed. Although I never partook of their food, nor did I exercise any vote of signing the petition, I was against the motion. Whilst they were noising about, they saw a steerage lady, after days of sickness (as our passage was very rough) eating a sprat, when they begged to have it in their dinner. Not being able to restrain myself any longer, I remarked—"during my boyhood in India I visited a lady relation of mine, seeing the beautiful moon, her baby boy cried, ' what is that, mamma ? ' ' the moon, my boy ' said the mother, when he said, 'I shall have it,' ' you can't have it because I cannot catch it for you,' replied the mother. I told them, ' you can't have it because in this high sea the crew cannot catch it, nor have they any on board the ship." This remark satisfied an anti-motionist and his party. But they all, some contemptuously and some earnestly, cried for a speech. I agreed to their request and delivered a speech. Having met with no obstacles (as a person whilst speaking might tumble on account of the rolling of the sea or he might be sick) I could undertake to speak, and God helped me during my first and second attempts on board the ship.

The steamer despite her disability made rapid progress, and brought us much earlier than we expected into the port of Liverpool, where Teutonic arrived only a few hours before us. I spent a night in a hotel and left Liverpool for London.

On my arrival in London, I met an Indian, who bitterly complained of the rigour of the English winter. I remarked had he experienced the American cold weather he would have never regarded England inclement. On this, his curiosity being greatly excited, he inquired whether I mitigated it by meat and warm port wine. He was greatly surprised to learn that rice sufficed to maintain my health and comfort and said, he had spent about £400 on port alone, still he experiences the rigorous inclemency of the climate.

The supposed necessities imposed by the climate, forces an Indian to find a ready apology for the drinking habits of the West. The unnecessary expenditure explains the problem of vast wealth, side by side with abject poverty of the majority of the Indian population, whose annual mortality from starvation is very great.

> " Ill fares the land to hastening ills a prey,
> Where wealth accumulates and men decay,
> The princes and lords may flourish or may fade,
> A breath can make them as a breath has made.

Whilst the laboring class in India is suffering from starvation, this man has spent £400 on warm port, under a misconception of its real nutritious value; and this instance is but a solitary grain amongst the infinities of the seaside sand. Whilst myriads, in India luxuriate in self-indulgence regardless of the bitter-biting anguish of his less favoured countrymen, this man has come over to this country to display his riches to the vendor of red-bottles.

The want of sympathy with poverty and suffering is the modern feature of the quasi-English; but the genuine orientalist of the days gone by, was keenly alive to the duties of hospitality and had universal repute for self-denying charity. The merchants of India, still support their traditional name for recognising the inequalities of fortune of mankind, and not unfrequently, have their names appeared, as princely donors, during famine.

Tradition affirms that there once lived a man named Karna, whose great generosity won for him the title "Data" generous. Once he entertained a priest who informed his host, that the supply of a large quantity of meat was essential to appease his hunger. The host consented and the guest further alleged that his meal must be of human flesh, so it was requisite that his only boy Brishakatu, should be sacrificed for that purpose. The host fettered by the obligation of the promise which was inviolable during Satwa, or truthful period, with a doleful heart sent for the boy. In compliance with the injunction of his father, the boy unaware of his fate made his appearance. The priest further added that the father himself should behead the child with willingness and alacrity, since any show of sorrow would convince him of his unwillingness to fulfil the obligations of hospitality. Under the threats of sacerdotal displeasure, the parents were compelled to kill their only child and cook his flesh. They then begged the inhuman priest to take his horrid meal. But the priest now alleged that soup was the principal dish of his dinner, and without soup he would refuse the meal. Plunged into the extremity of grief on account of the sacrifice, the host could afford no more congenial prospect than the wish that the guest should withdraw, although the angry departure of a guest was reckoned in those days, a source of misfortune. So he politely represented that all the meat had been cooked and that not a bit was remaining to provide soup. But the host was informed that the hostess intended to burn the head, and retain its ashes in a cinerary urn. The soup was prepared as the excuse was unavailing. The guest desired that four persons, the host and hostess and their guest, together with a boy from a neighbouring house, should dine together. To gratify the desire of the guest, the bereaved father departed, when to his great astonishment, he found his own boy was playing with the other children of the same age. He accompanied the boy to his house, when he saw the priest assumed the form of a god and said he visited Karna, with intent to try his fidelity and generosity and he had borne that in a manner far exceeding the expectation of the priest, who forthwith disappeared. The narration is but a fable but still it is the finest specimen of the illustrations current throughout India of unquestioned obligation to the sacred rites of hospitality.

Referring to the man of whom I have previously spoken, indulging in the port wine as a specific against the frigidity of English climate, I beg to say that I know a priest in India who is a total abstainer. When dying from the effect of a dangerous fever, owing to the prescription of a doctor, he took alcohol. On partial recovery, he found one Sunday, which is the great festive day of drunkards

throughout the world, a crowd in the heat of liquor created
great disturbance, upon which he slowly crawled to the
place and standing with the assistance of his stick, he
admonished them for their clamours and for their insatient
indulgence in intoxicating drink and exhorted them to
temperance. By this representation he simply wanted
them to shun all kinds of beverages and sow the seed of
beneficial actions.

The dying man, availing himself of the temporary
strength conferred under the stimulant, and successfully
combatting its use, is a spectacle unique in the history of
mankind. This is the marvellous temperance address in
its noblest aspect. It must not be supposed that all
temperance advocates are of such strength of mind. Too
frequently they, like the sign post at a cross road do
not take, but merely point the way to healthful prudence
and morality. I must confess to have met with such
advocates, in several parts of the globe.

With regard to the liquor question, I beg to say that
my conscience forbids my indulgence in such a liquid
which takes away the sense of a man. During my boyhood
I suffered from the effects of liquor; although I myself
was a total abstainer and will continue to be so as long as
the date of my life shall last; I had a house built at
Valuka, Kishnaghur, at my own expense and by my own
exertion. One night a drunkard crept in and set it on fire
during my besotted incapacity for carefulness. I escaped
with life but all my belongings were reduced to ashes.
Since then I have been residing in foreign countries and
the sympathy which I have enjoyed from the people of
several parts of the globe, has largely sufficed to ameliorate my memories of sorrow and afflictions ; I would have
been able to complete my studies long ago had my enemies
not interfered with my property. The memory of the
following story has induced me gladly to submit to all the
multifarious troubles and difficulties, knowing that on some
future day they will be superseded by some propitious and
opportune moment.

In antiquity there lived a great Indian potentate named
Sributsha. Being a very virtuous King he merited the

admiration of the universe. For this reason, " Shani," the Devil, determined to subject him to the trial of poverty. The following day his troops broke out in open mutiny, and set his palace on fire. Upon this unforeseen disaster he started, heedless of the place of his destination. After walking a few miles, he rested beneath a tree where, to his great astonishment, he saw his wife Chinta, who, as he thought, met her fate in the conflagration, appear with a bag of money. The pair started on their journey and arrived at the bank of a river diversified with beautiful flowers. There was no ferry to cross the river, save that one, in which a man was catching fish. On the request of the King, to take them across, the fisherman took them in, alleging the limited accommodation of the little vessel would not allow him to carry them with the bag, which could conveniently be ferried over in the second load. Hardly they sailed, leaving the bag behind, a black dog carried it off and the man and his boat disappeared, and the bed of the river became a dry land. They renewed their journey and reached a fine grove with a tank in its centre, where the men were employed in catching fish. On the application of the King they furnished him with two fish which were handed to Chinta, asking her to fry them for breakfast. Being absorbed in reflecting the loss of territory and the tragic disappearance of the bag, she forgot all about the fish, the one burnt to ashes and the other was half burnt. In her attempt to wash, the fish slid away, being restored to life by the Devil. The King on his arrival from a bath was greatly perplexed, with the astounding circumstances of their mysterious departure. The royal pair set out and reached the shop of a village carpenter, who assigned to him a commodious cottage at a moderate charge. To meet his necessary charge, he went to a neighbouring jungle, fetched wood and lived on the sale of it.

One day, during the absence of the King, the ship of a great merchant was aground in the river running at the foot of the village. The crew in vain endeavoured to dislodge it ; accordingly the Devil advised the captain to avail himself of the help of the wife of a carpenter (the King

H

was known here by this name). On the application of the captain she touched her, and the vessel began to move. Representing the great utility of the help of the girl on similar emergencies, the Devil succeeded in inducing the captain, to take her on board. So she was conveyed on board the ship, which subsequently set sail. The empty house greatly affected the King, who knew not to whom to apply and where to find the abducted wife. Dethroned, melancholy and unfriended as he was, he thought to put an end to his sufferings by seeking a shelter beneath the roof of a gentleman, who had been a great friend of him during his halcyon days of prosperity. The gentleman sympathized with his bereavement and showed the hospitality of allowing him to stay a few days only. Drawing was one of the methods employed by the King to beguile his leisure. On the wall of his temporary room he one day drew a peacock; the Devil gave it life and the bird swallowed a golden necklace. The guest being accused of the theft, was insultingly driven away. Subsequently he visited another friend, who being under the superstitious influences of the Devil and dreading his malignant power, sought to propitiate him by administering poison to the King from the effect of which he died. Two of his tame birds* seeing the corpse of their master placed on the outer premises of the house, restored him to life by means of medicinal herbs fetched from the wood.

He went to a deep jungle, built a cottage in the neighbourhood of a Cabila, a particularly sacred cow, and comfortably resided. He made some bricks, burnt them and temporarily piled them high by the sea-side in hopes of being able to erect a house of his own in future. In the evening, he spent his leisure-hour by observation from the pile. One day the crew of the vessel in which the wife of the unfortunate King had been carried away, observing a large pile of bricks almost unprotected, threw the man overboard, conveyed his only property and set

---

* Birds and beasts are far more reliable companions to the distressed than men, who are sure to forsake their master on the disappearance of his prosperity.

sail. The King was carried away by the waves and under-currents to a distance, when he was discovered by a girl who conveyed him to her house and nursed him until his recovery. Learning her kind hostess was in the employ of a royal family, he requested her to introduce him as an applicant for an engagement. On her recommendation, he was appointed superintendent of the wharf. One day during his official hours, he saw the same vessel which carried his wife away and which threw him overboard, and forthwith issued an order of her detention. On claiming the wife and the bricks, they were restored. Ample compensation was given by the captain for his outrageous actions. Now the Devil forsook him and the prince learned, with transports of joy and surprise, that the superintendent. of the wharf was no common man, as he himself was but a feudatory chief of the King. He made an apology for his not treating him with the necessary dignity and sent him to his kingdom. His subjects, being greatly oppressed by a tyrant dethroned and slew him on the approach of their rightful King. He assumed the sovereignty, built a magnificent palace and reformed the army and navy. The legend further adds, that when he was reinstated, he visited his false friends stated above. The murderer very kindly admitted him and desired him to live with him as long as he pleased and implored forgiveness for past action. The offence was forgiven but the King was wise enough not to reside with him any more. The accuser also received him cordially and in vain assigned a room for his residence. The King forgave his offence and went to the peacock for the necklace which was restored to its rightful owner. Thus the King spent the remnant of his life in comfort, happiness and peace.

Examples drawn from myths and fables are not necessary, to assure my readers that the trials of human life give birth to virtues, which otherwise could never be developed. Integrity is displayed only in the face of temptation; patience, fortitude and resignation are evolved only by suffering. Sympathy, philanthropy and charity can be appreciated only by him, who has been developed by poverty, misfortune and suffering.   Few men in health, appreciate the blessing, with which it is endowed but pain and disease caution us against the evil propensities of our life, and stimulate our gratitude for the immunity, which we enjoy.   My departure to the United States of America, proved a turning point in my career; but although my life's pathway has not hitherto been very rosily strewn, I am still hopeful if God be willing, of achieving the particular object, to which the whole of my life has been devoted.

www.ingramcontent.com/pod-product-compliance
Lightning Source LLC
Chambersburg PA
CBHW032355280326
41935CB00008B/581